Starting Your Own Business

Visit our How To website at www.howto.co.uk

At **www.howto.co.uk** you can engage in conversation with our authors – all of whom have 'been there and done that' in their specialist fields. You can get access to special offers and additional content but most importantly you will be able to engage with, and become a part of, a wide and growing community of people just like yourself.

At **www.howto.co.uk** you'll be able to talk and share tips with people who have similar interests and are facing similar challenges in their lives. People who, just like you, have the desire to change their lives for the better – be it through moving to a new country, starting a new business, growing their own vegetables, or writing a novel.

At **www.howto.co.uk** you'll find the support and encouragement you need to help make your aspirations a reality.

You can go direct to **www.starting-your-own-business.co.uk** which is part of the main How To site.

How To Books strives to present authentic, inspiring, practical information in their books. Now, when you buy a title from How To Books, you get even more than just words on a page.

2009 000 163

Starting Your Own Business

How to Plan and Build
Your Own Successful Enterprise

6TH EDITION

Jim Green

howtobooks

Published by How To Books Ltd,
Spring Hill House, Spring Hill Road,
Begbroke, Oxford OX5 1RX, United Kingdom
Tel: (01865) 375794 Fax: (01865) 379162
info@howtobooks.co.uk
www.howtobooks.co.uk

How To Books greatly reduce the carbon footprint of their books by sourcing their typesetting and printing in the UK.

First edition 1995
Second edition 1998
Third edition 2000
Revised and re-issued 2002
Reprinted 2003
Reprinted 2004 (twice)
Fourth edition 2005
Reprinted 2006
Fifth edition 2008
Sixth edition 2010

British Library Cataloguing in Publication Data.
A catalogue record for this book is available from the British Library.

ISBN 978 1 84528 420 6

Produced for How To Books by Deer Park Productions, Tavistock
Typeset by PDQ Typesetting, Newcastle-under-Lyme, Staffordshire
Printed and bound in Great Britain by Bell & Bain Ltd, Glasgow

NOTE: The material contained in this book is set out in good faith for general guidance and no liability can be accepted for loss or expense incurred as a result of relying in particular circumstances on statements made in the book. Laws and regulations are complex and liable to change, and readers should check the current position with the relevant authorities before making personal arrangements.

CONTENTS

LIST OF ILLUSTRATIONS

PREFACE

Becoming a successful entrepreneur is not only a rewarding and self-fulfilling experience, it's also a tremendous amount of fun. Many people equate the term entrepreneur with multi-millionaires running international conglomerates. Yet traders just down the street from where you live who make their living from retailing, plumbing, painting and decorating, electrical installation, building, floral arrangement, interior design, child minding, dentistry, chiropody, garden maintenance, insurance, image-making and a host of other things – all are entrepreneurs, and they get as much satisfaction from their enterprises as any multi-millionaires.

Entrepreneurship is an attitude, a whole way of life. When you choose to start your own business you are also choosing to become an entrepreneur, and to begin this new way of life.

Maybe you've already given some thought to striking out on your own but feel that the risks are too great, the timing not right, the economy too bad. You feel you'd never be able to raise the funds, you're too young/old/tired/retired, you're too unemployed/redundant/rejected – you're too whatever.

This book aims to help you decide whether you're right or wrong, whether you have what it takes to strike out on your own and stamp your personality on an enterprise of your very own making.

Let me tell you my own story. It was a cold wet Friday morning in November and for the last time I was walking the short distance from the car park to my little office on the hill. I was feeling my age, the money had almost run out and my wife was just days away from death. Thirty minutes later I had lost my job, my income and my car.

As I trudged through the rain looking for a taxi home I thought, 'You should be cracking up now.' But I wasn't. Instead, I was experiencing an inner peace I'd never felt before, coupled with a fierce determination to fight back.

And fight back I did. I also ceased to worry about *anything* from that day on. It was my personal road to Damascus, the dawn of realisation.

You will find many strands of 'fighting back' throughout these pages. Regardless of your personal circumstances this book will show you how to strike out on your own and get your life going again.

I've been an entrepreneur for a long time. I've won some and I've lost some but I wrote the first edition of this book while I was doing it yet again so that whatever wisdom it might contain would come fresh to the reader from current experience. Now 16 years on, as I complete my revisions for the sixth edition, I'm still at it: launching an ever-increasing shoal of virtual businesses online.

The contents are not about the mechanics of running a business. You won't find any mention of the complexities of the VAT system, how to compile your tax return, what qualities you should be looking for when choosing a solicitor or accountant. There are lots of excellent books around dealing with these matters, including some in this series. This book concentrates on the creative heart of business, on how to develop an exciting enterprise from the original germ of an idea.

If you do decide to become an entrepreneur may good luck and good fortune be yours all the way.

Jim Green

1
GETTING STARTED

Before you make a conscious decision to start out on the exciting journey that leads to entrepreneurship, it's advisable to take stock of yourself. See whether there are any mental blocks standing in your way, blocks that might hold you back in your endeavours. Identify these right now and get to work immediately on eradicating them.

WHAT'S HOLDING YOU BACK?

Something must be holding you back, or you wouldn't even have read this far.

I didn't spot my own mental blocks in time and it cost me my first successful enterprise. In my case it could be summed up as the mid-life crisis. For many of us it arrives at 40-something, for some earlier and for the real tough nuts, early 60s as retirement looms. In my own case it hit me like a thunderbolt at 50.

I was founder, chairman, managing director and majority shareholder of a highly successful advertising agency (lightning does strike twice). Blue chip accounts were our stock-in-trade. Many of them were institutional accounts where the money was safe, you always got paid on time, and you would have had to murder the chairman or his wife to lose the business.

Yet, the business I lost – not the individual accounts but the business I had conceived as a whole, worked long hours to build and for which I had spurned a substantial offer to sell just months before my dénouement. To this day I still have no idea why I turned down that offer because in the end I was relieved to hand over my company to a conglomerate for one pound sterling (I've still got it) just to get rid of the hassle and the £100,000 overdraft. Or so I thought at the time.

Why did I lose my business?

For years I asked myself that question daily and failed to come up with the real answer. The reason was that I was looking in all the wrong places.

- ☐ I blamed it on the hassle. (*Untrue* – I loved the hassle.)
- ☐ I blamed it on the overdraft. (*Untrue* – the business was solid, the overdraft manageable.)
- ☐ I blamed it on key management. (*Untrue* – they all contributed something to the business.)
- ☐ I blamed it on domestic pressures. (*Untrue* – although my dear late wife had been stricken by an irreversible illness, she was coping better than me at the time.)

☐ I blamed it on Old John Barleycorn. (*Untrue* – I ended up in counselling only to find that this wasn't the root cause.)

So what really went wrong?

The truth came to me quietly that day I trudged through the rain looking for a taxi and the answer was the key to the inner peace I was also to discover. I had simply *given* it all away.

At the age of 50, with a successful business, substantial personal cash reserves, a small mansion, three prestige cars, I just blew it. In short, I lost my confidence and ran away. Why?

☐ *I simply wasn't ready for success.*

Not only did I lose my business, my livelihood, my personal fortune, I was also subjected to a seven year investigation by the Inland Revenue which I wouldn't wish upon anyone (they were so thorough in their endeavours, they ended up *refunding* me over £14,000).

LEARNING TO HANDLE SUCCESS

When do you learn to handle success? Easy. Just as soon as you work out what's stopping you. If you happen to be 20 when you crack this, so much the better, but for many it takes a little longer to face up to the truth.

So what ails you? Now's the time to find out, evaluate the situation and get your life going again. Could it be one or other of the elements of the modern version of the three 'Rs' (redundancy, retirement, rejection)? Is unemployment getting you down? Are you fed up hearing people tell you you're too old? Does everyone say you're too young? Or are you just stuck in a rut?

OVERCOMING THE MENTAL BLOCKS

Let's examine each mental block to see how it might affect your particular circumstances.

Are you finding redundancy tough to handle?

Redundancy is rotten, isn't it? One day you're one of the crowd, the next you're out on your butt in the freezing cold. The employer may give you a sweetener but it's rarely generous. It soon disappears on urgent calls from the bank manager, mortgage lender and sundry other claimants. Instead of staying home feeling miffed, wouldn't it be more satisfying to get out there and *do* something about your future? After all, you *have* got one.

Has retirement come too early for you?

If you fail to plot the route through your late years accurately, you may be in for some heavy weather ahead. Some people make the mistake of retiring far too early, have lots of cash, lots of time on their hands . . . and a terrible feeling of frustration. Even if you're fit and well, you'll still need an outlet for your energy. What better than something of a commercial nature?

If you don't need the profits, you can always give them away to a deserving cause. Read on.

Is constant rejection getting you down?

I've been there many times. After I lost my business I worked for several years as a home-based marketing consultant and was doing pretty well until the recession began to bite in October 1990 when I suddenly became a dispensable luxury to my clients. They could no longer afford me and day by day I received 'Dear John' letters. However, one of these clients seemed to think I still had something to offer. He put me on his payroll. That lasted twelve months, then he went spectacularly bust.

Following a period of totally unprofitable activity I sold advertising space as a self-employed rep for a national publishing concern. After a while they offered me full-time employment as a contracts negotiator. Then they got rid of me, and their top management, as they too proceeded to go bust in an even more spectacular way. Not very impressive, is it? Read on.

Do you feel helpless in unemployment?

Then for your own peace of mind, *don't*. There's a vast amount of practical help to be found once you start looking in the right places. I'm not being crass when I say this. I've been unemployed and managed to fight my way out of it once I learned to look in the right places for help. Read on.

Who says you're too old?

No one has yet dared say that straight to my face but I'm fairly sure many have thought so. So what? They're wrong and I can prove it.

Who says you're too young?

They're wrong too, so wrong. The future of the country lies squarely in the hands of its young citizens and you are *never* too young to start learning your trade as an entrepreneur.

Are you just stuck in a rut?

Maybe you are currently in a well paid, secure salaried position but bored out of your skull. Then *do something about it.*

Spend some time *right now* checking out your own mental blocks; list them starting with toughest and working your way through the remainder. Now create an initial action plan for eradicating all of them.

FIGHTING BACK

Finding out what is really holding you back often takes some time, and a good deal of soul searching. Again, the answer may come to you in a flash. In my case it happened the day my employment was terminated. After years of looking in all the wrong places, suddenly everything clicked into place. Within the space of a few hours I had not only identified my own particular core problem but was fighting my way back to recovery.

□ The gathering clouds of personal tragedy had brought me the answer. *Worry* was what had been holding me back. The route to recovery was to create a business of my own in the industry I had just been dismissed from and to develop that business free from the fear of worry.

This soul destroying emotion had been eating away at me all my life: not overtly in what I said or did, but subconsciously before I even got around to thought, speech or deed. Worry was my addiction and I simply couldn't leave it alone. It had enshrouded all the plans that had gone before and as a result tainted their development.

Building the path to recovery

I was good, *very* good, at what I did in the industry I had been thrown out of earlier that day: contracts negotiation. I also had a working knowledge of all the other aspects in which I had not been actively involved. With over 30 years' hands-on experience in the advertising industry, I reckoned I had at my fingertips all the makings of a successful publisher.

I determined there and then – without capital or resources – to create my own publishing business and to do so free from the fear factor. Not helping you much all of this is it? Bear with me a little longer.

I decided to put the matter of lack of capital and resources on the back burner meantime and to concentrate on the immediate essentials of creating a basic plan initially for survival, then for success.

My shopping list comprised the following:

□ Sign on the UBO for the first time in my life.
□ Inform all of my previous clients of my intention to start again on my own.
□ Find some money to live on.
□ Get myself mobile again.
□ Locate a cost-free training course on information technology.
□ Create the beginnings of my business plan.
□ Look again at personal financing for my enterprise.
□ Discover if I had any friends who might consider investing.
□ Establish the route to public sector funding.
□ Brush up on my entrepreneurial skills.

How I achieved all ten of these initial goals and how their development contributed to my master plan is the basic subject matter of the chapters to follow. My hope is to offer you an insight into what it takes to become an entrepreneur. I did it, and so too can you.

What's held you back so far?

Now that you've heard my confession, let's have a quick recap on what might be *your* mental block to launching your very own enterprise.

Too old?   _____
Too young?   _____
Too tired?   _____
Too retired?   _____
Too broke?   _____
Too redundant?   _____
Too rejected?   _____
Too much to hope for? _____

However you may view yourself right now, there's no telling how far you can go if you really put your mind to it. For the moment, please take my word for this statement. Later, if you persevere, you'll discover the truth of it for yourself.

Too old?

Says who? You're really only as old as you have a mind to be.

Too young?

Rubbish. Go for it. You may not get a second chance.

Too tired?

Then wake up. Creative activity is happening all around you. Join in.

Too retired?

Then start over again and get back in the driver's seat.

Too broke?

So was I. In Chapter 4 I'll tell you how to remedy the situation.

Too redundant?

So no one's ever going to employ you again. So what? Get started and hire yourself. It'll be the best job and the best boss you've ever had.

Too rejected?

There's only one way to get rid of it. *Forget it.* But only after you've forgiven those who are doing the rejecting. They don't know your side of it and, even if they did, they probably wouldn't understand.

Too much to take on board?

Can't be or you wouldn't still be with me.

You'll need a plan before you start

The beginning of my plan was the little shopping list outlined above. Perhaps it might be no bad thing if you were to do likewise. Just jot down the basic things you have to do to get yourself going again.

Let's see how I got on ticking off the initial items on my list.

Signing on

That was an experience. The young lady behind the desk enquired about the occupation I'd just lost, then took a quizzical look at me as she said: 'Oh, there's not much call for that around here. Shall I put you down for clerical vacancies?' Charming.

Informing my clients

Easy. I rattled out a standard letter on my ailing Amstrad, personalised it, told everyone the truth and asked them to keep the kettle warm as I'd be back on their doorstep with my own business within the year.

Finding the money to live on

Not so easy. My visit to the UBO established the fact that I was not entitled to unemployment benefit. I had insufficient NI contributions, having been in a full-time job for less than two years (I was previously self-employed). So for the next six months I lived on Social Security. It didn't bother me. I'd paid plenty into the system for 40 years prior.

The DSS money was topped up by £1,000 I raised from selling personal odds and ends, and following extensive correspondence with the Inland Revenue I managed to obtain a tax refund. It was very tight for six months but I managed somehow.

Getting mobile again

I had no spare cash and HP was out of the question, so I hawked a diamond ring I'd bought my wife many years before. It had cost £5,000. Mappin & Webb in their generosity and my desperation gave me £1,150 for it. That allowed me to invest in a little red Lada which gave me excellent service for the next half year.

Cost-free training

The UBO were less than helpful. Too old to qualify for free training, they reckoned. So I bounced around in my Lada from one training house to another without much success. Finally I came across one where the chief trainer gave me the age limit for recruits with his first breath. I sawed five years off my age and was admitted that very afternoon to an Information Technology Course. The 'training' was non-existent but I spent the time

LAUNCH PAD

1   Find an idea

2   Get some cash together

3   Think about a trading name

4   Research the market

5   Study the competition

6   Write a business plan

7   Locate a training programme

8   Choose a partner

9   Investigate potential funders

10   Talk to the bank manager

11   Source initial equipment

12   ......

Fig. 1. Getting on the launch pad.

poring over manuals and engaging in interactive, tutorial dialogue with a stream of delightful young Americans. The course ran for 13 weeks, five days a week and was excellent value at 0 per cent APR. I was computer literate at the end. A few months later I received a cheque for £25 for being top student (that means the one that got a job).

Maybe the first few items of your initial list will show up something like this:

1. Find an idea.
2. Write a business plan.
3. Find some seed capital.
4. Source the mainstream finance needed.
5. [and so on].

CHECKING YOUR READINESS

What's *really* holding you back?

- ☐ Are you willing to do something about it?
- ☐ Are you worried about becoming really successful?
- ☐ Are you still worried about being considered too old or too young?
- ☐ Are you still worried that your unemployment status will count against you?
- ☐ Are you bothered about feeling broke?
- ☐ Are you ready to draw up a plan?

CASE STUDIES

Tom's first steps to freedom

Tom was made redundant nine months ago. He had been suffering from acute depression until recently when he finally made his mind up to do something about it. Tom had often thought about going into business for himself; since it now seemed clear that no one else was likely to offer him a job in the near future, he concentrated all his efforts on planning the launch of his own enterprise. Tom was a printer by trade, so a small jobbing print shop was what he set his sights on.

Tom had taken his first two steps on the journey towards entrepreneurship: he faced up to what was troubling him and he started to make a plan.

Paul and Hazel team up

Paul is 19 and his girlfriend Hazel is his junior by one year. Just weeks after leaving school Paul secured a job as an apprentice cook in the canteen of the local Council offices. He loved his job but because of cutbacks (or so they said at the time) he was made redundant on his 18th birthday. He hasn't worked since.

Hazel on the other hand has never had a job since leaving school, but not for the want of trying. She hasn't been wasting time though. She's attended several youth training schemes including one on business administration which she found most enjoyable.

On the way back from signing on one day, Hazel stopped in her tracks, tapped Paul on the shoulder and said,

'Hey, we could do that. We could start our own business.'

'Do what?' said Paul.

Hazel pointed to a mobile fast food shop on the other side of the street.

'Don't be daft. We don't know anything about running a business and anyway, we've got no money.'

'We could always get some. We wouldn't need much and my dad is forever saying you can always get money for a good idea.'

'Fat lot of good it's done him, he's still on the dustcart.'

'But we could do it. You can cook and I know about business administration...'

John and Colin pool their ideas

Neither John (55) nor Colin (52) needed to work for an income but what they did need was a job. They had both taken early retirement from well paid occupations with index linked pensions.

Retirement was great to begin with, but as time wore on boredom set in. The days were a drag and both men were really frustrated.

One afternoon John and Colin compared notes on the bowling green and decided that they still had plenty to offer and what they needed was a meaningful outlet for their energies.

After tossing a few ideas around they came up with the notion of supplying their services to the community...but how?

ACTION POINTS

1. List any mental blocks you feel may be holding you back in thinking seriously about setting up on your own.
2. Focus on the one mental block that may be the key to the others.
3. Try drawing up a strategy to overcome this.
4. Make a stab at an initial plan of action.
5. Select the most difficult aspect and write down how you intend to resolve this.

2
FINDING IDEAS

You'll need a really hot idea to get your enterprise going, but that's no great problem. There are hundreds of great business ideas, if you know where and how to look for them.

LOOKING RIGHT IN FRONT OF YOU
- ☐ Which subject did you enjoy most at school?
- ☐ Were you good at what you did when you were in full-time employment?
- ☐ Did you enjoy what you did for a living?
- ☐ If you are currently in employment, are you happy doing what you do?
- ☐ Could you do it successfully without any supervision?
- ☐ Are there aspects of your work you could improve upon if only someone asked for your advice?
- ☐ Does what you do (or did) make money for your employer?
- ☐ Is there still a market demand for the product or service?

Alarm Bell

Do it now. Look right in front of you and provide your own answers to the questions posed above. Taking action now will clarify your thinking and stand you in good stead to tackle the twists and turns that lie ahead.

Moving ahead by changing direction

Think, too, about how you might use your experience in launching out in business but taking a body swerve in direction – poacher turned gamekeeper. I did just that; for many years I had bought advertising space in large quantities for my clients. Then I changed to selling it in even larger quantities to subsidise the production of my publications. The experience gained in one aspect of the industry paid off handsomely on the other side of the fence. You might well find a similar application for your experience.

CASHING IN ON CHANGE

The economy is crying out for entrepreneurs of all ages, irrespective of social standing and net worth. The days of conglomerate inward investment as a safe route to economic progression are over. What's needed now are thousands of home-grown well thought out start-ups to foster recovery and engender the re-growth of our economy. The whole national and international economy is changing at a huge rate, affecting every market for private and public sector products and services. Business opportunities are everywhere.

Maybe you don't want to go back to what you did, maybe you have no idea what you'd like to do or maybe you just want to keep your options open. But here are some starting points for coming up with ideas.

Entrepreneurship training programmes

Waste no time in approaching your local Skills Funding Agency. Ask for details of which programmes they sponsor relating to **entrepreneurship**. These programmes are orchestrated by commercial concerns but the high running costs are met by central and local government agencies (a measure of official concern about the absolute necessity for growth).

Apart from being the best option for sourcing business propositions that are thoroughly researched, tried, tested *and* work, these programmes will also provide you with a real grounding in the **skills** you'll need to run a business.

CARVING A NICHE

A market in its entirety is too broad in scope for any but the largest companies to tackle successfully. The best strategy for a smaller business is to divide demand into manageable market niches. Small operations can then offer specialised goods and services attractive to a specific group of prospective buyers. There will undoubtedly be some particular products or services you are especially suited to provide. Study the market carefully and you will find opportunities.

As an example, surgical instruments used to be sold in bulk to both small medical practices and large hospitals. One firm realised that the smaller private practices could not afford to sterilise instruments after each use as major hospitals do, but instead simply disposed of them. The firm's sales representatives talked to surgeons and hospital workers to learn what would be more suitable for them. Based on this information, the company developed disposable instruments which could be sold in larger quantities at a lower cost. Another firm capitalised on the fact that hospital operating rooms must carefully count the instruments used before and after surgery. This firm met that particular need by packaging their instruments in pre-counted, customised sets for different forms of surgery.

While researching your own potential, consider the results of your market survey and the areas in which your competitors are already firmly situated. Put this information into a table or a graph to illustrate where an opening might exist for your product or service. Try to find the right configuration of products, services, quality, and price that will ensure the least direct competition. Unfortunately, there is no universally effective way to make these comparisons.

A well-designed database can help you sort through your market information and reveal particular segments you might not see otherwise. For example, do customers in a certain geographic area tend to purchase products that combine high quality and high price more frequently? Would your potential small business clients take advantage of your customer service more often than larger ones? If so, consider focusing on being a local provider of high quality goods and services, or a service-oriented company that pays extra attention to small businesses.

If you do target a new niche market, make sure that this niche does not conflict with your overall business plan. For example, a small confectionery processor that makes chocolates by hand cannot go after a market for inexpensive, mass-produced chocolates, regardless of the demand.

 No one knows your aspirations better than you; no one knows quite as much as you about the niche in which you intend to operate. Now is the time to establish *what you don't yet know* and fill in the blanks.

ACQUIRING COMMERCIAL SKILLS

Here's a list of the topics to be found in a typical prospectus for a public sector sponsored training programme:

Team building
New business planning
Markets and market selection
Product identification
Support systems for start-ups
Financial planning
Sourcing public sector financing
Sourcing private sector financing
Sourcing proven ideas
Legal aspects
Producing your business plan
Launching and managing your new venture

The particular course I happened upon was called 'The Entrepreneurship Programme' and was superbly run by my now good friends Andy McNab who initiated the programme, Will McKee, Les McKeown (entrepreneurs in their own right) and Dennis Murphy, programme manager par excellence. They're not paying me to say nice things about them. But I owe them all. The 26 week course cost me just £150 and I reckon I got 100 times that value out of it.

Do yourself a favour and enquire now.

WORKING ON YOUR SELF-ESTEEM

You won't find age, social standing or net worth a barrier. The only thing that might debar you is low self-esteem. Get working on that now if you think you have a problem.

All you will have to do is show willing to learn and participate with your fellow entrepreneurs on the course. You should be at a real advantage because this book will give you a practical insight into many of the topics you'll encounter.

CHOOSING A TRADING NAME

This is a vital question you will need to address as soon as possible. List as many ideas as you can before deciding on the name your enterprise is to trade under. Getting it right from the start is essential – you don't want to have to change it after a few months or a year. There are a few house rules to become familiar with before proceeding further. In essence, the ideal trading name should meet these five requirements:

Five guidelines

1. No more than seven letters in the composition of the core word in the title, preferably five.
2. No more than three syllables in pronunciation of the core word, preferably two.
3. The name must look *and* sound right.
4. It must fit the purpose of the enterprise.
5. It must be legally acceptable.

Let's examine each of these points in detail.

Five to seven letters

Why? Because the shorter the better for memorability *eg* FOCUS (5), HABITAT (7). Look at the big names in retailing: COMET, ARGOS, INDEX, VOGUE, B&Q, HOMEBASE. Keep it short and simple. As long it complies with the other four guidelines you should be on a winner.

Two to three syllables

Why? Your trading name must roll off the tongue as sweetly as honey off a spoon, for example, Pri-mark (2) Fo-cus (2), Hab-i-tat (3). Avoid tongue twisters at all costs if your name is to be famous one day. There are some well known exceptions but none of them breaks your jaw. MARKS & SPENCER (13 letters, 4 syllables) but most people say M&S or Marks & Sparks. McDONALDS (9 letters, 3 syllables).

Sounding and looking right

Get 1 and 2 right and your chosen name will sound right. But it's got to look good, too, and lend itself to graphic development. That's why a maximum of seven letters is desirable. It will be easier to put it into a graphic context.

Fitness to purpose

This seems obvious enough and hardly worth comment, but while driving through Cheshire I happened upon three examples which blew away this particular guideline:

Mistletoe Heating & Ventilation
Thistledown Hydraulics
Verabill Transport

What does Mistletoe have in common with heating and ventilation or Thistledown with hydraulics? Does anyone know? As for Vera and Bill (bless 'em) why don't they find another name. How about 'Stagecoach'? (Sorry, too late – this beautifully simple, apposite tag has already made Ann Gloag rich and famous.)

Whatever, avoid generics like Acme and Ajax. They have become hackneyed and convey nothing.

Using your own name

This is quite acceptable and makes a lot of sense if you're setting up as a consultant of one kind or another. But keep it simple. Not 'Charles A Farley Marketing Services', but 'Farley Marketing', for example, using the core words to best effect.

Legally acceptable

When you've finally decided on a name, make sure that (a) it conforms to legal requirements, and (b) no one else is already using it. You can easily do this yourself (by completing the necessary forms and paying a small fee) or by instructing your solicitor. Don't despair if you discover that someone else is already trading under the name of your choice.

The trade classification may be different. I wanted to call my company Focus Publishing but the search indicated another company with that name. Further investigation confirmed they were graphic designers whereas my business is publishing. All I had to do was effect a slight change, so I opted for Focus Publishing International as it had always been my intention to have the company trading overseas in due course.

There's a lot in a name. Get it right from the beginning: it could become expensive to change it later.

CHECKING YOUR READINESS

- ☐ Where is the first place you will look for an idea for your enterprise?
- ☐ Why would you say start-ups are so important to the economy?
- ☐ Where can you learn to become an entrepreneur?
- ☐ Why is good self-esteem so valuable? Will you do something about yours if it's at a low ebb?
- ☐ Why is it vital to get the right trading name? How many letters and syllables will yours contain?
- ☐ When could it be OK to use your own name?
- ☐ Will the name fit the purpose of your enterprise?
- ☐ Will it be legally acceptable?

CASE STUDIES

Tom finds a training programme

Although Tom was 90 per cent certain that he wanted to open a print shop he decided to keep his options open and began hunting for a public sector sponsored entrepreneurship programme. He didn't have far to look because within days he spotted a full page advertisement in his local paper giving complete details of the prospectus, starting date and entry requirements.

Tom wasted no time in applying. The following week he attended an interview for selection. He was pleasantly surprised at how well it went. He seemed to be just the sort of chap they wanted to recruit and although he had to answer many questions not once did the interviewer ask Tom for his age. Tom was 49 and reckoned that might be against him. He was wrong.

By being selected for this start up training programme (although he didn't appreciate the fact at the time) Tom was going to benefit greatly from the commercial skills he would acquire and the opportunity of seeking out a partner for his new enterprise.

Hazel's dad 'weighs in'

'But no one will take us seriously,' said Paul.

'Yes, they will if we've got a plan,' replied Hazel.

'What kind of plan can we come up with to raise some capital? Anyway we've got nothing to start with but our dole money.'

'I can write us a plan, I learned how to do that on the business administration course and Dad's promised us £500 to get us going. I talked it over with him last night and he thinks it's a great idea.'

'Business must be booming on the dust...'

Opportunity knocks for John and Colin

The day following their chat on the bowling green John and Colin made an appointment to visit the local Social Services department to see whether there was any call for their idea of community service. Much to their surprise they found there was. One of the biggest problems in the area was locating a reliable concern who would contract to ferry elderly and disabled citizens to and from various social gatherings the department had arranged on a weekly basis. It was recommended at the meeting that John and Colin should visit the local Skills Funding Agency to enquire whether there was any assistance on offer for such a project.

ACTION POINTS

1. Write a brief statement on what you're really good at. How would you enjoy doing it for a living? Could you make money out of it in a business of your own?
2. Assuming that you do not wish to set up a business in the precise industry in which you gained your experience, how could you put that experience to good use in a different direction?
3. Start finding out as much as you can about courses sponsored by Central Government which specialise in 'Setting Up Your Own Business'.
4. Make a list of the commercial skills you would like to acquire.
5. Think of six possible trading names you could use.

3
CREATING A WINNING BUSINESS PLAN

You can't start too early creating your plan for achievement. Start *now*. Don't even wait until you've settled on an idea. That may take a little time and no bad thing either. Best to get it right from the beginning. 'But how can I start writing a plan for my business when I'm not absolutely sure yet what I'm going to be doing?'

Fair comment, but what you can do is to *plan* for your Plan.

PLANNING AHEAD

No one really likes writing reports, and that basically is what your business plan will be, a report. It will be a report to keep you focused on your goal, a report which will gradually shape up as the means of impressing investors, raising the necessary capital and turning your idea into reality.

The first thing is to learn how to create a winning plan, a plan that is well researched and grows in value each time you work on it.

Get all the help you can in the beginning. There are some very good books on the subject. If you've never written a business plan for yourself before, I would recommend you invest in a copy of *The 24 Hour Business Plan* by Ron Johnson, published by Hutchinson Business Books at just under £20. It is excellent value, but I'm not suggesting you attempt to write your plan in 24 hours, and neither does the author. Read the book through once and then use it as a constant reference manual as you progress your own plan. It will lead you gently through the intricacies of composing a *winning* plan and give you a grounding in the structure required. If you would rather use a paperback, see Matthew Record's *Preparing a Business Plan* (How To Books).

Focusing on the end result

Developing your business plan should be fun. It will get the creative juices flowing and keep your mind focused on the ultimate goal: turning your idea into a practical, profitable enterprise of your own.

Even if you haven't finally settled on an idea yet, you'll find that as your learning curve accelerates so too will a decision on the idea that will change your life for the better. The inspiration will soon flow.

A winning plan calls for a high degree of introspection. As you progress you'll find yourself facing up to reality quite readily. When you start committing your thoughts to paper the good, the bad and the ugly aspects of any business idea come to light fairly quickly. This can prove unsettling at first but you'll soon find that you are addressing the negative factors with increasing confidence and vigour. Certain aspects will call for an immediate re-think, further research or perhaps total rejection. Now's the time to find out and put matters right. There will be no scope for dummy runs once you begin trading. Basically, that's what will make your plan a winner: examining, honing and polishing all the components before you fix them firmly into place.

Remember, if you're less than 100 per cent convinced about the finished article, what chance will you have of impressing potential investors?

Example: Focus Publishing International

For the record, I started to put my business plan together the very day I was made redundant and worked solidly on it every day for seven months. Although I'm no accountant I provided initial projections for cash flow and profit & loss spanning three successive years. It will really pay you to do this even though you are rather unsure of many of the figures. Use trial and error. Practice makes perfect, and you can always call on professional help later on.

When I applied to join the 'Entrepreneurship Programme' I did so with three key aims in mind:

- □ to brush up my entrepreneurial skills
- □ to discover a route to public sector funding
- □ to find a management accountant to be a partner and shareholder in my enterprise.

I was successful in all three of my aims and it was my partner-to-be who restructured my rough financial projections into a meaningful, attractive proposition for potential investors. But he had the initial raw material to work on and only I could have produced that. I knew the business.

MAKING SURE THE PLAN IS YOURS

Whatever shape your winning plan eventually takes, make sure it's got *your* hand on it. You may need help with the overall structure and that's OK but don't be tempted (even if you have the money) to rush out and assign all this hard work to a management accountancy practice specialising in the preparation of business plans (not unless your idea has enormous investment potential). If not, you're liable to get a pull-down menu version adjusted to suit the profile of your idea – and you won't get much change out of £2,000.

It's your baby and you must see it through all the way. It's you and *your* team who will one day have to put the plan into practical effect: not a professional adviser.

No matter how rough hewn at this stage, jot down a few initial thoughts on your goals, objectives, aspirations, concepts for the enterprise, competition, and whatever else springs to mind – but do it now.

YOUR BLUEPRINT FOR SUCCESS

The plan you are conceiving for your business is your blueprint for success. Plans are great things. They show you where you're going, what to do and how to do it when you get there. Make no mistake, your business plan isn't just designed to get you started and raise some working capital. It's going to be around for a long time and you'll want to review and update it regularly to take account of the unexpected twists and turns along the way. That's the beauty of it. When you have a plan, you can legislate for change. Without one you're sunk. You'll be an explorer in a jungle without a map.

While no two business plans are alike, they all have similarities in structure. The temptation can be strong (you'll find this out very quickly) to crash on and produce a tome as thick as *War and Peace*. Avoid this temptation. The fewer the pages in your final document the better. A dozen or two may suffice. Quantity will never impress an investor, it's the quality of the idea they measure together with their conception of how likely you will be to turn it into a reality.

The format you must work to is simplicity itself. You deal in turn with each of the component parts in a logical and progressive manner, much as you will do when you're actually putting them all together at the outset of your enterprise.

Putting the pieces together

Here's your initial scheme. Ironically, it begins with the one exception to the advice in the paragraph immediately above.

Structuring the executive summary

You will write this only on completion of the entire plan but it must appear at the very beginning. Why? Because potential investors are unlikely to progress further in their reading unless you give them an immediate 'handle' on what you and your idea are all about. This is also the most difficult section to write and usually takes a few attempts before you can satisfactorily mould it. It shouldn't be any longer than a couple of pages so a great deal of thought has to go into what headings stay in and what ones are left out. No one knows the subject matter better than you. Only you can write it.

Your management team expertise

If you're going to use your plan to raise capital, you'll need to give details of the status, qualifications and experience of your key personnel. It is extremely difficult to attract mainstream investment nowadays for a one-man band. It's possible, but the conditions are restrictive. However, don't be put off. Your initial team could acceptably comprise yourself and one other person: spouse, partner, boyfriend, girlfriend, son, daughter, niece, nephew or, as in my own case, an equity partner.

Your concept

You understand your business idea inside out but does anyone else have a clue what it's all about? Summarise your concept in writing on just one page. Explain in detail exactly what it is. Leave emotion out of it. Stick to the facts.

How your concept works

Many good business ideas fail to get past the starting gate simply because the originator can't or won't elaborate on how the idea works in practice. Once again a single page will suffice, but be precise. In my experience, the inclusion of a simple diagram or flowchart works wonders.

Your business objectives

Your objectives must be detailed, well thought out and thoroughly researched. They should include not only the objectives for your embryo enterprise but also your own personal aspirations for the venture and how you plan to achieve the goals you've set. You'll want to list them as they apply to the short, medium and long term. There's nothing difficult or mysterious about any of this, it's simply a matter of doing it.

What do you know about the market?

You'll need to do some research before you pen this section (even though you reckon you know all there is to know about your market). Markets and market trends change constantly and rapidly, sometimes overnight. Into which sector or sub-sector of the market will your product/service fit? Will it be sold on through conventional channels or will it require specialised distribution? These are just some of the questions you'll be answering.

Researching the competition

There's no show without Punch and where there's no competition, there's unlikely to be any business around either. Find out who your competitors are. Which of them are the strongest in your catchment area? Discover all you can about them and record it faithfully in your plan – even if some of it scares you.

Describe your product

Describe in detail – in not more than one page – exactly what your product or service is. Summarise where it differs from similar propositions, what the benefits are to the end consumer, and why you believe you're on a winner.

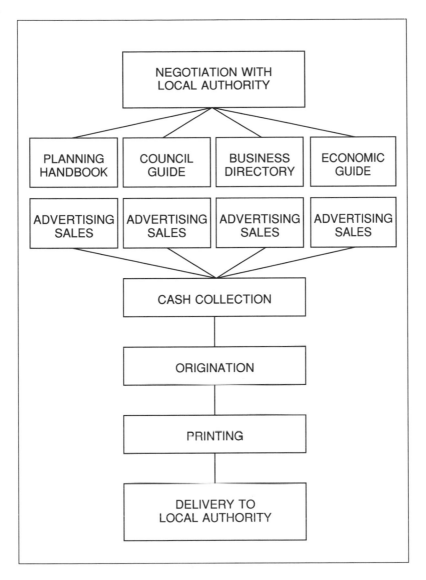

By producing a simple flowchart (or schematic) like this one, you can make it easier for others to understand what your venture is all about. It works best if you can illustrate an element of uniqueness *ie* in this example the cash is collected *before* pressing the button on producing the product.

Fig. 2. A typical format for a business plan.

This is essential work and it's never too early to make a start. Have a stab right now at producing your own schematic. No matter how sketchy at the outset, it will galvanise your mind into ironing out the wrinkles as you progress.

Packaging your proposition

Here's where you wrap 'Concept', 'Methodology' and 'Product/Service' into the unique package you'll be offering your customers. Even one slight improvement on what the competition offers might be sufficient to give you an early edge. Will it be discounting, overall pricing policy, unique marketing, or what?

Evolving your sales policy

The marketing plan for your idea will determine your sales policy and whether you require to invest in a sales force. Will you be selling through wholesalers, agents, retailers, off-the-page or door-to-door?

Marketing your business

A great deal of rubbish is spouted about this key business function and usually by people who should know better (see Chapter 6). Suffice to say, keep your marketing simple and relevant to your idea. There's no mystique about the subject.

Your unit production/sales forecast

Whether you're planning to manufacture or to provide a service, you'll still want to complete this section: the number of knobblewockers you intend to knock out weekly – or the number of assignments you are forecasting to complete.

Your production costs

Again, whether manufacturing or supplying a service, you'll be incurring production costs and, before you get to your bottom line, you'll have to make estimates for them.

The strengths and weaknesses of your idea

Even though you believe you're on a winner, you may just have re-invented the wheel. There are bound to be some weaknesses in any proposed new operation. Jot them down as well as the strengths. If you don't do it now, some potential investor will do it for you just when you least expect it.

GETTING HELP FROM THE PUBLIC SECTOR

When you get around to seeking financial backing for your project, you'll be asked to make out a case for it. Here's just the place to start.

- □ Will you be creating additional jobs in your area?
- □ Would you be prepared to recruit unemployed labour?
- □ Would you offer training?
- □ Do you envisage doing business outwith your local economy?

If you can answer 'Yes' to these four questions, you'll be a prime candidate for public sector assistance by way of grants and/or 'soft' loans. More of this in Chapter 4.

Funding your enterprise

You will be demonstrating projections over three successive years for cash flow, profit & loss and balance sheet. If you're not an accountant, call in some expert help. Whatever, be honest and practical. Don't delude yourself or tell porkies. Why funders require fantasy forecasting for years two and three I'll never know but they insist on it.

Useful appendix/appendices

A very useful section into which you can house all the other pieces of back-up information that don't seem to fit in too well elsewhere (CVs, price lists, budget workings, etc).

GETTING HELP FROM THE BANKS

Contact the Small Business Adviser at your nearest main clearing bank branch and request a copy of their respective Business Start-Up Packs. Barclays and Natwest are particularly good. I cannot recommend these superbly constructed documents too highly. Study the contents assiduously and they will provide you with an easily digestible insight into all you need to know before putting your plan together. They approach the exercise from different angles and by reading both you'll benefit from two sets of expertise. It's a pity they're not always so forthcoming at handing out the cash but more on that subject later and how to deal with it.

It sounds like a great deal of hard work, this blueprint for success. It is but there's no other way. Once you get started, you'll find your imagination taking off; all sorts of things that didn't make too much sense before will now start falling into place. Try it, you'll be surprised how good you will become at it.

CHECKLIST

- ☐ Plan ahead for your business plan.
- ☐ Focus on the end result.
- ☐ Write the plan all by yourself.
- ☐ Summarise the content and position it accordingly.
- ☐ Explain exactly how your business idea works in practice.
- ☐ Describe your business objectives.
- ☐ Define the marketplace.
- ☐ Research the competition.
- ☐ Produce a clear description of your product or service.
- ☐ Describe the key elements of your sales policy.
- ☐ Develop a plan to market your enterprise.
- ☐ Summarise both the strengths and weaknesses of your idea.
- ☐ Make out a case for public sector assistance.
- ☐ Show how you will fund your business.
- ☐ Describe the market, its characteristics and current trends.
- ☐ Show precisely where your product or service fits in.
- ☐ If it slots into a particular niche, describe this sub-sector.

CONSTRUCTING YOUR 'BLUEPRINT FOR SUCCESS'

You can't start too soon preparing the business plan that will crystallise your thoughts and bring your idea to the attention of potential investors. Imagine the overall template as the trunk of a pine tree with the bold headings as branches and the bullet points as pine needles. Here's how it works:

Executive summary

- ☐ Brief description of the business.
- ☐ Target market segment.
- ☐ What makes your enterprise different from competitors?
- ☐ Why should anyone invest in it? (credibility factors: track record, management team's expertise, etc).
- ☐ How much finance is required, nature of funding (loans, grants, equity participation)?

Management team expertise

- ☐ Experience, qualifications, specialist knowledge of each of the founding members. Summarise to meet the requirements of your particular venture.

The concept

- ☐ Just what is your idea?
- ☐ Explain it fully but briefly.
- ☐ If it's brand new, prove its practicality.
- ☐ If it's been around for years, who else is doing it?
- ☐ What's different about your idea?
- ☐ Is there a gap in the market for it?

Methodology

- ☐ Describe on just one page exactly how your idea works in practice, step by step.
- ☐ Use a simple schematic to illustrate this.

Objectives

- ☐ List your objectives for the enterprise: personal and business, long and short term.
- ☐ Now show how you intend to realise these objectives.

Market

- ☐ Even though you think you know your market inside out, research it again fully before committing this section to paper.
- ☐ Describe the market, its characteristics and current trends.
- ☐ Show precisely where your product or service fits in.
- ☐ If it slots into a particular niche, describe this sub-sector.

Competition

- ☐ List the main competitors in your immediate catchment area.
- ☐ Detail their product ranges and illustrate where they differ from yours. If they are superior, say so; if they're not, explain why not.
- ☐ Give a breakdown of current competitive market shares.
- ☐ If you perceive a gap in the market for your particular product or service, guesstimate how you think the competition will react on your entry into the market.

The product

Some schools of thought have this section appearing before 'Market' and 'Competition' but I think it's best unveiled after you've talked about these aspects.

- ☐ Devote just one concise page to its description.
- ☐ If it's different from competitive alternatives, say so.
- ☐ If it's superior, say so.
- ☐ If it's inferior, say so and then explain why you believe there's still a market for it.
- ☐ List the benefits to the end consumer.

Packaging the proposition

- ☐ Wrap concept, methodology and product into the benefits package you'll be offering your customers.
- ☐ One slight difference makes all the difference.
- ☐ Will it be discounting?
- ☐ Will it be incentive marketing?
- ☐ Will it be added value service?

Marketing your business

- ☐ Keep your marketing simple and relevant to your product or service.
- ☐ Avoid a convoluted approach.
- ☐ You should be planning a launch brochure.
- ☐ Think carefully before allocating monies for advertising.
- ☐ Plan for cost-free PR exposure.

Evolving the sales policy

- ☐ Your marketing strategy will determine the sales policy.
- ☐ Will you require a sales force?
- ☐ Will you engage the services of a major wholesaler?
- ☐ Will you be selling off-the-page?
- ☐ Will you sell by direct mail?

Units forecast

- ☐ If you're manufacturing, this is essential.

☐ Even if you're not, you'll still want to record the assignments or projects you are forecasting to complete.

Production costs

☐ Whether manufacturing or supplying a service, you'll be incurring production costs.
☐ Record your monthly forecasts.
☐ Will you be buying from only the one source?
☐ Will you be using several suppliers?
☐ Do you anticipate special terms with some of these suppliers?
☐ Make sure you record everything before you get to the bottom line.

Strengths and weaknesses

☐ Elaborate on the strengths of your scheme.
☐ No matter how brilliant, there are some weaknesses. Jot them down faithfully before someone else does it for you.

The case for public sector assistance

☐ If you feel you may have a case, here's the place to state it.
☐ Will you be employing local labour?
☐ Would you employ and train unemployed people?
☐ Is your business manufacturing based?
☐ Would you be interested in a local authority nest unit?
☐ Will you be trading outwith the local economy? (If you can answer yes to these questions, you'll be in line for public sector assistance.)

Financial projections

Be precise in both your forecasting and your funding requirements:

☐ Profit & loss over 2/3 years.
☐ Cash flow over 2/3 years.
☐ Balance sheet for years 1, 2 (and 3).
☐ Start-up funding requirement.

You'll need some help with this. Make sure you ask for it.

Appendix

☐ CVs for yourself and your partner.
☐ Orders or written 'promises'.
☐ Anything else of relevance that doesn't fit in elsewhere.

CASE STUDIES

Tom's plan takes shape

Tom's days were no longer empty and depressing. In fact, some days he found himself working longer hours than when he was in a job and enjoying himself into the bargain. He'd borrowed some books on business administration from the public library and was making notes from the sections relevant to launching his own particular enterprise.

The initial sessions on team building and planning which Tom attended at his start up programme were also proving to be both interesting and useful. Although he hadn't started to write it yet, his business plan was already beginning to take shape in his mind.

What excited Tom more than anything else was the fact that the skills he had acquired working for wages in the printing trade over 30 years were now being employed fashioning a venture of his very own. What's more, he could see that he could make money out of it – much more money than he'd ever made before.

Hazel and Paul disagree

'So, what do you think?' asked Hazel.

'Just a minute.' Paul was on the final page of the business plan Hazel had prepared for their mobile fast food venture. It contained twelve pages in all. It covered matters such as concept, trading name, the partners' respective qualifications and experience, territory of operation, start-up costs, profit margins, turnover and cash flow projections. 'Great, when do we start?'

'Not before we've laid our hands on £2,500,' replied Hazel.

'That's the bit I don't agree with. We don't need as much as another £2,500 to get us going. We could buy an old banger and a secondhand microwave and save a packet.'

'No. That wouldn't be saving, it would be wasting money. What if they both keep breaking down? We'd be out of business in no time.'

'No we wouldn't, I can fix things as good as anyone. You know I can.'

'Sure, but we need to keep your time for making up those lovely sandwiches and pastas. We can't have you working as a mechanic as well.'

'Point taken. You're the boss.'

'No I'm not, we're partners. Wait a minute though. Someone has to be in charge...'

'Like I said, you're the boss. Shall I call you Sir?...'

John and Colin visit the Skills Funding Agency

'So, gentlemen, tell me what you have in mind.'

John and Colin were in the offices of the Skills Funding Agency and had just been introduced to one of the Business Development Executives. John explained the bones of their idea and the outcome of the meeting with the Social Services. Colin had prepared a rough business plan. He passed around copies and gave the executive a run through on the salient points.

There would appear to be several chances of help: 'booster' grant, soft loan, and places on a refresher course on business administration for John and Colin. Another meeting was arranged for a few weeks hence when the executive would report back on progress.

EXERCISES

1. Visit your local public library and bookshops. Browse through the shelves for books on business administration and in particular, business planning. Choose the one(s) best suited to your particular needs.
2. Visit your local bank branches and obtain copies of their respective business start-up packs.
3. Make a start on assembling the bones of your plan, using the guidelines provided in this chapter.
4. Having completed (3) draft an executive summary to put at the front of your eventual business plan.
5. Make out an initial case for public sector assistance.

4
FUNDING YOUR ENTERPRISE

GETTING YOUR HANDS ON SOME SEED MONEY
You'll need seed money to begin with and then, later, working capital to get your enterprise up and running.

START-UP COSTS
Every business is different, and has its own specific cash needs at different stages of development, so there is no generic method for estimating your start-up costs. Some businesses can be started on a shoestring budget, while others may require considerable investment in inventory or equipment. It is vitally important to know that you will have enough money to launch your business venture. To determine your start-up costs, you must identify all the expenses that your business will incur during its start-up phase. Some of these expenses will be one-time costs such as the fee for incorporating your business or the price of a sign for your building. Some will be ongoing, such as the cost of utilities, inventory, insurance, etc.

Identifying your costs
While identifying these costs, decide whether they are essential or optional. A realistic start-up budget should only include those things that are necessary to start that business. These essential expenses can then be divided into two separate categories: fixed expenses (or overhead) and variable expenses (those related to producing sales for the business). Fixed expenses will include things like the monthly rent, utilities, administrative costs, and insurance costs. Variable expenses include inventory, shipping and packaging costs, sales commissions, and other costs associated with the direct sale of a product or service.

Using worksheets to speed the process
The most effective way to calculate your start-up costs is to use a worksheet that lists all the various categories of costs (both one-time and ongoing) that you will need to estimate prior to starting your business. There are tools to assist you in performing that task and you will find them at the following websites. Use whichever you decide works best for you.

http://www.bplans.com/common/startcost/index.cfm
http://www.businessknowhow.net/bkh/startup.htm

Example: Focus Publishing International

I wish I could tell you that I found this easy. But I didn't. The only income I had at the time was from Social Security and the only spare cash I had left was barely enough for basic living expenses. The situation was dire for someone hell-bent on launching a business in six months' time. Even worse, the targeted launch date coincided with the time I reckoned I had to start earning or risk going under personally.

To attract sufficient working capital from an amalgam of commercial and public sector funding sources, I needed to raise a minimum of £10,000 as seed money or founder's equity, whatever you'd like to call it. (My partner had a similar brief.)

Show time: I did some serious soul searching, a little lateral thinking and a lot of praying. The £10,000 cash I needed urgently and didn't have. I had a house with just enough spare equity to cover the requirement but this was the final bastion – and anyway, how could I possibly demonstrate ability to repay? Did I have any friends or relations who might help out? I did but this was a route I didn't want to take. Some people don't mind accepting this kind of assistance. I do.

What else did I have? – Two annuities on which I had somehow managed to keep up the contributions through thick and thin. They were only two years away from maturity and intended as a substitute for a pension (some pension). I decided to cash them in and lose a small fortune in the process. Then I thought again.

Magic, lateral thinking or inspiration

What if I could borrow £10,000 against the final maturity values but *defer* repayments until the due maturity dates (which were within days of each other)? If this were possible then all I had to do was keep up the premiums which I had been doing anyway for eight years and clear off the respective loans in one go when both policies matured.

My initial approaches to the sources concerned were bounced out of court but with persistence, obduracy and persuasion I managed to convince them eventually that I was a good bet for such a deal.

My policies had been performing better than I realised and the loan cheques I received totalled £12,500, leaving me a comfortable balance to add to my budget for living expenses.

There's always a way

Chances are you're not as hard-pressed as I was then but if you are, take heart. There's *always* a way if you're determined enough to think it through to actuality.

So what are the limited key options available to you for raising some seed capital for your enterprise?

☐ personal resources
☐ insurance policies

- □ annuities
- □ spare equity on your home
- □ friends and relations
- □ bank loan (but you can't go back for more and your chances of getting an overdraft when you most need it are negligible).

Not a lot up for grabs, is there? But there's enough. If you really want it badly enough, want to strike out on your own, you'll find a way.

Alarm Bell

You have just looked at six core possibilities for raising seed capital but your personal circumstances might throw up several more; if so, write them down and then rearrange the list in preferential order.

GETTING OUTSIDE FINANCE

Whatever the nature of your idea you'll almost certainly require additional investment from external sources to transform it into a reality.

Where do I start looking?

There are only two acceptable, safe options: private institutional and public sector sources. What you should aim for is an amalgam of both but with the emphasis on public sector assistance. We'll look at this in more detail a little later.

Who do I talk to in the private sector?

This will depend very much on the intended scale of your operation. If you're thinking small to begin with, then the best place to start is your bank manager but do not expect too much enthusiasm or understanding from that quarter. All banks have had their fingers burned in commercial lending over recent years and they tend to be scathing about approaches centred on start-up projects. Not very encouraging is it? Don't despair, though. We'll leave your bank manager to the very end.

On the other hand, if your idea is on the grand scale you ought to be having early conversations with venture capital houses and circulating your business plan around such as 3i, Charterhouse, Morgan Grenfell and the like. But these institutions will only take you seriously if your investment requirement has a minimum base of £500,000. If you're thinking big, talk to them.

APPROACHING THE PUBLIC SECTOR

A great deal is available from the public sector if you go about it the right way. This is the area you should concentrate on first. Why? – Because you'll get a friendly ear to your initial overtures and an honest appraisal of your project.

So what is available?

Grants are great

The great thing about grants is that you don't have to pay them back. They come in all shapes and sizes: employment, training, marketing are among the ones most readily available for start-up projects. Don't be shy about asking. A roll-up package of these three grants can be very useful in your early trading days. In certain areas you will qualify for a New Business Grant for yourself if you are unemployed as I was. Employing others who are on the dole equally qualifies your enterprise for grants ranging up to 60 per cent of wages and National Insurance contributions for the first 26 weeks. Assistance with training is also available with grants up to 100 per cent for the first year. Marketing grants (available only in certain areas) range from 30 to 50 per cent.

Soft loans

Go for these first before you even discuss arranging a facility with your bank manager (I'll tell you why later). Now don't get too excited about the term 'soft'. There are no soft touches among the people you'll be dealing with and you'll have to pay back the money sometime. These loans are 'soft' only inasmuch as they are structured on very competitive terms, unsecured up to £10,000 and usually carry a capital repayment holiday of three to six months.

If you can satisfy the funders' criteria (which are not punitive) try to achieve much of the finance you will need from this area.

Free initial training for yourself

Even if you already consider yourself well versed in information technology, don't fail to take advantage of one of the various public sector sponsored technology training courses available to approved start-ups in many regions of the UK. The one my company opted for wasn't entirely free but for an investment of just £500 we got £1,500 worth of training plus brand new computer hardware and software with a combined price tag of £2,000. Getting our hands on £500 in the early days of trading wasn't easy but the effort expended paid off handsomely.

APPROACHING POTENTIAL FUNDERS

Clearly, you won't even consider approaching any funder until you're 100 per cent happy about your business plan. You will need to feel confident that you will be able to field any questions that may arise during initial discussions – and arise they certainly will.

Let's assume your venture will be on a small to medium scale, and that the financial section of your plan has clearly identified the working capital requirement for the first 12/18 months of trading. You ought also to have made a stab at how this funding would be best and most readily achieved.

Example 1

A snapshot for a total investment package of say, £100,000, could look something like this if you set out to raise it exclusively from commercial funding sources:

Requirement	£100,000
Financed by	
Founders equity/Loans	£ 50,000
Term loan/Overdraft facility	£ 50,000*
Total finance	£100,000

*Totally secured by collateral

Example 2

Take the same package but change the lens for the snapshot to include public sector assistance:

Requirement	£100,000
Financed by	
Founders equity/Loans	£ 25,000
Public sector grants	£ 20,000
Public sector unsecured loans	£ 40,000
Bank overdraft	£ 15,000
Total finance	£100,000

Which deal are you going for?

The ratios between the two equations say it all. Dealing in the commercial sector alone you'll be doing well to achieve 50/50. Mix in public sector assistance and you will have additional numbers to play around with.

Example 3

If you think this is all a bit far fetched, let me show you now what my partner and I achieved on a total investment of £70,000, starting with bus fare only in my pocket:

Requirement	£70,000
Finance obtained	
Personal equity	£10,400
Partner's equity	£ 9,600
Public sector grants	£21,000
Public sector unsecured loans	£25,000
Bank overdraft	£10,000
Total finance	£76,000

Yes, we ended up with £6,000 more than bargained for in public sector assistance but still had to arrange for a £10,000 bank facility for reasons which I'll explain shortly.

My personal equity stake in the company came by way of borrowing against annuities and no bank would grant us an overdraft without back-to-back collateral. I had no money left to spare and I didn't have any in the first place. Solution? I borrowed another £10,000 on a credit card (no questions asked) and stuck it in a high interest savings account as collateral against an overdraft we barely needed to draw on anyway.

What did I say? There's always a way.

Now that you know why we're going to leave the bank manager to the very end, let's establish the batting order in your approach for funding:

Public sector

But make no approach until you've studied everything on offer in your local area; made a value judgement on which grants would be applicable and whether you have sufficient grounds for qualifying; which and what levels of unsecured loan assistance your embryo business could afford in the very early days. Do your homework thoroughly. Leave nothing out of your 'needs' reckoning but ask for not a penny more than your plan calls for (despite my experience).

Sources of Public Sector Assistance

According to your status and location visit the website most appropriate to your specific requirements from those listed and described in Appendix 1.

Commercial sources

If your venture is small to medium, this means the bank. Go here last and only when you've got the rest of your funding in position, *ie* your own investment, your partner's investment and public sector grants and loans. Banks only lend to start-ups on totally secured, belt and braces conditions. You've got to get one of them interested but take only as little as you need.

THE PLAN THAT WILL FIX YOUR FUNDING

Follow these suggestions to the letter. They're based on my personal experience. They worked for me and they'll work for you.

Step 1

Expect and allow for many meetings with your chosen public sector funders. Patience is the name of the game. The initial enthusiasm of their new business teams will be quickly replaced by seemingly sanguine indifference from the investment managers. Don't be put off. On the contrary, take careful heed of any suggestions they put forward about your overall plan. It's all part of the game. They know better than you the route to successfully enacting your grant and loan applications. Listen to them and they'll help you, although you may not think so at the time.

Step 2

Accept from the outset that it's all a bit of a game and there's a hidden agenda that no one's going to tell you about (except me). Don't worry, the pieces will all eventually fall neatly into place as long as you are totally honest in all your conversations with the public authority people. But here's a really key tip.

☐ *You will require to convince all of them individually and collectively that your plan is sound and worthy of public sector assistance.*

That's a tall order considering that it's well nigh impossible to get them all together at the same time for a corporate meeting on your proposition.

Here's what you do to convince them all individually and collectively without getting them all together face to face.

(a) You're confident about your new venture. Now prove that you have reason to be confident. Go out and get some orders confirmed in writing (or if you can't manage that yet, some promises). Circulate the news to all concerned by fax.

(b) Zero in on the one funder with whom you feel most comfortable. This will almost certainly be the one who'll get the brownie points when you get your funding. Make this person your first point of call. Keep up the pressure until you get a letter confirming a deal. You'll get that letter.

(c) Send faxes to the others advising them of the funding breakthrough.

Get one to say 'Yes' and the others will fall into line rapidly.

Step 3

Now you can go to the bank manager. In fact you'll have to go to the bank manager because the offers of grant aid and loan assistance you have received from the public sector will be conditional on your ability to raise the balance of your funding from the *commercial* sector by whatever means you can. It's no good suddenly finding this balance from your hip pocket or producing a bundle of cash from a friendly aunt. Those are the rules and there are no exceptions.

But now you know something no one else is going to tell you, so you can go funds-sourcing with a degree of confidence.

The 'Fax that'll Fix the Funding'

Use and adapt the example on page 36 to secure your funding.

To: Ralph Graves, Anywhere Skills Funding Agency
From: Ed Wynn, Sensor Batteries
Subject: Grant & Loan Applications

New Business Gains

Yesterday afternoon I completed negotiations on two very important pieces of new business representing a combined contribution of £45,000 to the first month's trading performance of Sensor Batteries. As work begins immediately on both of these assignments, I am sure you will appreciate the urgency of an early and favourable decision on my company's Grant & Loan Applications.

The good news doesn't stop here...

I have several other tenders moving along rapidly to maturity and expect to be able to report back shortly with news of further acquisitions.

Regards

ED WYNN

PRESENTING YOUR CASE

Wrapping up the package

How you present yourself and your case for assistance is key to obtaining early and favourable decisions all round. How you finally wrap your package and present it to the decision-makers is equally vital.

There was a time not too long ago when you only heard of advertising agents making presentations. Now, it seems, everyone's doing it. But you can learn a lot from the way ad agents go about it. Their presentations are very professional, very fast and get to the heart of the matter with a touch of style. They are also very expensive.

Five tricks of the trade

Now, I'm not suggesting you invest a bundle of money in your presentation but there are some tricks of the trade worth embracing:

1. Make sure that the final version of your business plan is professionally executed, is free of errors (literal and numerical), has a distinctive cover and is securely bound. If you don't have access to a word processing facility, rent one.

2. Have copies of your proposal in the hands of all the participants at least two weeks prior to each meeting.

3. If you are unused to presenting to others, practise beforehand on family or friends. Don't waste time feeling awkward about it. Ask them to be objective in their appraisal of your performance.

4. Speak up when you get there. It's your show. You're on and you're centre stage. Don't leave it to the others to open the dialogue or cover up awkward gaps in the conversation later on.

5. Above all: keep on the lookout for buying signals and when you receive an offer which is favourable to you, *shut up*, pack up and go away. Don't even wait for a cup of coffee or you may find yourself going suicidal and talking your way out of the deal you've worked so hard to put together. It happens.

CHECKLIST

- ☐ Describe how you will obtain seed money to get you started.
- ☐ List various sources you could approach to raise seed capital.
- ☐ Look at ways you might attract external funding.
- ☐ Name potential supply sources in the private sector.
- ☐ Make out a case for public sector assistance.
- ☐ Describe what is readily available from the public sector.
- ☐ Highlight the core advantage in grant funding.
- ☐ Describe 'soft loans'.
- ☐ Locate free training opportunities for skills improvement.
- ☐ List all the sources for public sector assistance.
- ☐ Explain why you would contact the public sector first.
- ☐ Explain why you would leave the banks until last.
- ☐ How would you present your case for assistance?
- ☐ Why is it important to package it properly?

CASE STUDIES

Tom seeks an experienced partner

Tom's initial plan was to go it alone in his new enterprise. However, he was some weeks now into his entrepreneurial programme and already discovering several good reasons why it was necessary to be taking seriously the matter of looking around for a partner.

To begin with, maths was never Tom's strong point. He was going to need some professional help when he got around to preparing financial forecasts for his business plan. Moreover, once the business was up and running, who would look after the bookkeeping and administration? His wife didn't seem too keen (anyway she was in regular employment).

It had also occurred to Tom that his own initial cash injection for the business might not be enough to attract external funding. What he needed was an equity partner with specialist skills in management accounting and administration – and some capital to invest in the enterprise.

He decided to start looking for one.

A guarantor for Paul and Hazel

Paul and Hazel had their first meeting with the Young People's Learning Agency. The agency couldn't offer direct assistance but commended their initiative and made an appointment for them to visit a government agency specialising in youth incentive schemes. Our entrepreneurs met again later in the day.

'Guess what? I showed Dad our plan and told him about the meeting, and guess what?'

'What?'

'He's offered to go guarantor for a £1,000 bank loan! We've got an appointment with the bank manager for tomorrow afternoon.'

'That's great news. Aren't dads just wonderful? He must own that dustcart . . .'

Colin and John agree their finances

Colin had by now made good progress on refining the business plan for 'Comely Coaches', the name under which they agreed the partnership would trade. John had located a nearly-new 12 seater minibus which was well within budget, and costed out several other essential pieces of equipment. They had also agreed the capital to be introduced into the business by each of them. It was to be a 50-50 split.

All in all Colin and John were well fixed for the next meeting with the Skills Funding Agency which was just a few days away.

ACTION POINTS

Tackle each of the following points according to whether you already have a business idea or whether you're still thinking about it (in which case use a hypothetical scenario).

1. Make out an itemised list of your initial seed capital requirement and then determine how you will go about fulfilling the requirement.

2. What private and commercial sources could be available to you for external investment in your enterprise? Draw up a list.

3. Which public sector sources within your area could you approach for financial assistance by way of soft loans and grants? Draw up a list.

4. Evaluate your total funding requirement by (a) commercial investment only and (b) a mix of commercial and public sector funding.

5. Write the copy for your own personal 'fax that'll fix the funding' (see page 36).

6. Draft two brief presentation scripts intended for (a) commercial funders and (b) public sector funding sources.

5
PLANNING AHEAD

Before you launch your new business you'll want to be planning ahead for every eventuality. It may be you'll need a partner to make it work; now's the time to be thinking about this. You'll certainly want to measure up the competition and you'll need to think about premises and systems.

CHOOSING A PARTNER

If (like me) you're a loner by nature, you may be wondering why I include choosing a partner as a vital step in starting up. I include it for one reason and one reason only. If your new venture calls for outside capitalisation, you won't get it unless you can show clear evidence of team building in your plans. Lending sources in both the private and public sectors are mustard on this condition nowadays. A friend or relation prepared to invest some money in your idea is helpful but not nearly enough. You still won't get the cash unless your prospectus includes a strong section on management expertise. This does not mean to say you have to join up with several partners. Just one will do as long as he or she has specialist skills that complement your own. Who knows, a member of your family might fit the bill.

Finding the right partner

Your best bet is to sign up for a public sector start up training programme. I joined my course with that as a prime aim and I was successful in achieving it. But it didn't just happen; I had to work at it. The programme gave me a platform from which I could view and assess the various alternatives. That, as I perceived it, was the core benefit in joining. I was going ahead anyway with my plan for a new business, but I knew that to attract the necessary external finance, I also had to attract a suitable equity participating partner. These programmes are composed of an enviable mix of skills and experience. Whatever you're looking for is almost certainly bound to be available if you can just get the chemistry right.

The qualities to look for in a partner

There are four specific areas you'll want to investigate thoroughly when considering who is going to run with you in your new enterprise.

Integrity

Very difficult to assess in advance but make every effort to do so. He/she is hopefully going to be around for a long time to come, so be absolutely certain the successful candidate has lots and lots of this essential quality.

Complementary skills

For example, if you are the one who's going to be flying the nest every morning looking for business, you'll want to have someone reliable back at the office doing the books, conceiving and implementing systems and generally attending to all other matters of administration.

Experience

Establish right from the outset that your selected partner has a quantifiable track record in performing all the skills you need but don't have personally. Academic qualifications are fine up to a point but nothing really equals practical experience.

Solvency

If you are to attract the external finance you've identified as critical to your new business, your chances of success will be much greater if your partner is also investing in the seed funding. However, what some people say they will do and what they will actually do on the due date can vary dramatically. Make quite sure of the candidate's solvency and net worth before committing yourself to any deal. Don't be afraid to ask. It's your own future you'll be risking if you don't.

Choosing a partner: points to consider

1. Make out a list of the ideal qualities you would be looking for in a potential partner to join you in your new enterprise. Add to the list outlined in this chapter.

2. Think of six different ways you could go about finding a suitable partner.

3. Having evaluated your own commercial skills what complementary skills would you require in the chosen candidate?

4. Is there a family member, friend or colleague who might be worthy of serious consideration?

> **Alarm Bell**
>
> Study the four points again but this time take notes as you go through each of them. When you've finished, ask yourself, 'Do I really **need** a partner to get my intellectual property, my enterprise, up and running?'

CASE STUDIES: GOING INTO PARTNERSHIP

Tom looks around for assistance

Tom had now completed the first rough draft of his business plan. It was evident that for his new venture to be on steady ground from day one, he had insufficient cash available for seed capital. Tom was using what was left of his savings and redundancy payment but both had been seriously depleted during his months of unemployment.

Tom had also completed his initial sourcing for an equity partner. It hadn't proved too difficult after all; on the start up programme were several management accountants (some still employed, some not) and he'd struck up an acquaintance with each of them. Following deliberation he made his mind up to approach the one who best met the qualities he would be requiring in a financially participating soul mate.

He outlined his proposal to his colleague, handed over a copy of the plan and asked for a reaction within a week. Seven days later Tom had found his business partner, Paula (33) an unemployed management accountant. Paula now went to work on Tom's roughly hewn financial calculations to get them into shape.

Hazel's bank guarantee

The meeting with the bank manager went well (as well it might with Hazel's dad putting up the collateral for the loan) and immediately afterwards our intrepid entrepreneurs visited the offices of the Young People's Learning Agency) for a discussion on how best they might obtain the balance of their funding.

'As you can see from the business plan,' said Hazel to the new business executive, 'we need £3,000 in total to get us up and running. My Dad's already given us £500 as seed money, we've got a loan of £1,000 from the bank which Dad again is guaranteeing, so we're shy of £1,500. Can you help us?'

John and Colin get the good news and the bad news

Back again at the Skills Funding Agency with their updated plan and costings, John and Colin discussed the possibility of financial assistance from the public sector for their project.

The Business Development Executive explained that he had good news and some bad news for them. The bad news was that because 'Comely Coaches' was a project solely devoted to community service and unlikely to have employment growth potential, the best on offer was therefore a grant of £1,000 from the European Social Fund. Neither John nor Colin regarded that news as a body blow.

The good news was that the executive had discussed their plan with a local philanthropist who liked what he heard and had requested an early meeting with both of them.

MEASURING THE COMPETITION

However innovative the idea upon which your new business plan is based, someone else has thought of it before you.

Learning to live with competition

You could have invented a cordless toaster that runs on fresh air, butters and marmalades its produce and then sweeps up the crumbs. Someone's bound to be marketing something similar just around the corner. But don't let that put you off. Competition is the spice of business life. In fact, without it there would be very little creative activity in your marketplace.

Finding out as much as you can

Right from the start it will pay you to find out as much as you can about the people with whom you'll be jousting for orders. How do you go about this intelligence gathering? Easy. Many of your competitors are unable to contain themselves every time they're on a roll, they will employ expensive PR consultants to broadcast the news in the journals of your trade. We are not necessarily talking about large conglomerates who can afford this sort of indulgence. Many small concerns who can't afford it also employ public relations specialists. So, right from day one, subscribe to the key trade papers and start a cuttings service of your own. Don't pay anyone else to do this for you. Do it yourself, it's an excellent discipline.

Asking the clientele

Another good and reliable way of keeping up to date with competitive activity is to ask your customers. They won't mind. If they're getting good service, they'll tell you. If not, they'll also tell you, and there is your opportunity.

What sort of activity should you be monitoring in particular?

Checking your competitor ranges

Look early and carefully at the range of products/services marketed by each of your competitors. Do they vary much from yours? If so, how much and in what ways? Be honest and detailed in your appraisal. Are they better than you at some things? Would it pay you to adjust your range and come into line with the best on offer from the competition?

Checking operational areas

Dig deeply and establish who's doing what on your patch. It's not necessarily the biggest who gets the lion's share. Concentrate on the activities of the local market leader in your field and try to find out what makes them tick. Have they been around a long time? Is it their pricing policy, their marketing? Or do the rest of the competition think they've got it sewn up and just leave them to it? (There might be an opening here.)

 This is something you could do straightaway; find out all you can about a local competitor who is already established in the niche you intend to enter and dominate in time as market leader...

Deciding your prices

This is always rather a problem when you're starting out. The temptation can be strong to start with suicidally low margins or to take on assignments on a fee-based structure that you haven't a hope in hell of making any money out of. Try hard to avoid this route. You may have to turn down some business in the process but you must start the way you mean to go on: giving good service for a fair return. Don't be rushed into giving it all away just to get a few orders. Be patient.

Monitor your competition rigorously on their pricing policies. They've been at it longer than you, they've made their mistakes and learned from them. When you're tempted to undercut, think long and hard before you do. You may have to live with the painful effects of your impetuosity for a very long time.

Distribution channels

This may or may not be an issue depending upon the nature of your enterprise. If it is, study the distribution patterns of the competition before committing finally to the methods you will use. It could be very expensive if you don't get things synchronised from the beginning.

Establishing market shares

You might find this information easy to come by. I didn't. The industry I operate in is very much of a 'closed' nature (though I did manage eventually to acquire what I needed). Whatever, you need to find out, but remember it's only your immediate catchment area you're bothered about. You'll find a way.

Promotional activity

- ☐ Does your competition advertise heavily?
- ☐ Which media do they use?
- ☐ Do they exhibit at trade or consumer shows?
- ☐ Do they run incentive schemes for the trade?
- ☐ Do they operate premium offers for end users?
- ☐ How much do they budget for promotion?

You'll need reliable information on all these activities before you plan your own albeit limited programme.

Strengths/weaknesses of the competition

No matter how you may perceive your competition initially – or indeed how they perceive themselves – there will be well defined strengths and weaknesses in their structure which you must become acquainted with. You may not discover this intelligence for some time, and not at all without a lot of delving and observation. But when you do, it will be of immense value to your embryonic venture. Emulate their strengths, and try to capitalise on and learn from their weaknesses.

Putting your knowledge of the competition to work

When you've gathered together all this accumulated intelligence, put it to work on your behalf. Study the findings carefully. Pick out the core elements and concentrate on them as you start to prepare your own initial strategic marketing plan. This way you will learn to discipline yourself always to be aware of the competition and their marketing activity.

Questionnaire: how ready are you to face the competition?

☐ How much do you know about the competition for your idea? _____

☐ How much can you find out? _____

☐ Where's the best place to start asking? _____

☐ What knowledge do you have of the ranges the competition offer? _____

☐ What are their areas of operation? _____

☐ Do you know their pricing policies? _____

☐ Do you know the market shares? _____

☐ What sort of promotional activities does the competition undertake? _____

☐ What are their strengths and weaknesses? _____

☐ How would you put your accumulated knowledge to work? _____

COMPETITIVE ANALYSIS

Business takes place in a highly competitive, volatile environment, so it is important to understand the competition. Questions like these can help:

1. Who are your five nearest direct competitors?
2. Who are your indirect competitors?
3. Is their business growing, steady, or declining?
4. What can you learn from their operations or from their advertising?
5. What are their strengths and weaknesses?
6. How does their product or service differ from yours?

Start a file on each of your competitors including advertising, promotional materials, and pricing strategies. Review these files periodically, determining how often they advertise, sponsor promotions, and offer sales. Study the copy used in the advertising and promotional materials, and their sales strategies.

What to address in your competitor analysis

☐ **The names of competitors**. List all of your current competitors and research any that might enter the market during the next year.

☐ **A summary of each competitor's products**. This should include location, quality, advertising, staff, distribution methods, promotional strategies, customer service, etc.

☐ **Competitors' strengths and weaknesses**. List their strengths and weaknesses from the customer's viewpoint. State how you will capitalise on their weaknesses and meet the challenges represented by their strengths.

□ **Competitors' strategies and objectives**. This information might be easily obtained by getting a copy of their annual report. Conversely, it might take analysis of many information sources to understand competitors' strategies and objectives.

□ **The strength of the market**. Is the market for your product growing sufficiently so there are enough customers for all market players?

More ideas for gathering competitive information

□ **Internet**. The internet is a powerful tool for finding information on a variety of topics.

□ **Personal visits**. If possible, visit your competitors' locations. Observe how employees interact with customers. What do their premises look like? How are their products displayed and priced?

□ **Talk to customers**. Your sales staff is in regular contact with customers and prospects, as is your competition. Learn what your customers and prospects are saying about your competitors.

□ **Competitors' ads**. Analyse competitors' ads to learn about their target audience, market position, product features, benefits, prices, etc.

□ **Speeches or presentations**. Attend speeches or presentations made by representatives of your competitors.

□ **Trade show displays**. View your competitor's display from a potential customer's point of view. What does their display say about the company? Observing which specific trade shows or industry events competitors attend provides information on their marketing strategy and target market.

□ **Written sources**:
general business publications
marketing and advertising publications
local newspapers and business journals
industry and trade association publications
industry research and surveys
computer databases (available at many public libraries).

FINDING THE RIGHT PREMISES

You will have already given serious consideration to premises in putting together your business plan and initial budget. You may have decided, as I did, to operate your venture out of a room in your own home (or your partner's) for the first few months of trading. There's nothing wrong with that. It conserves cash and is quite acceptable nowadays to most funders. You obviously can't go on that way for ever, but it will allow you some valuable breathing space before making what may well be the single biggest decision you will face in expenditure and commitment in your new enterprise.

There's another way to begin operations before committing to a lease and I recommend you give it serious consideration. It works like this...

Getting help from the public sector

Local Authority Business Centres frequently offer start-ups a flexible deal. Typically, you can opt for renting accommodation and secretarial services on a short-term basis or, if you prefer, an accommodation facility for mail, messages and secretarial help. Their terms are very reasonable and you can cancel the arrangement anytime it suits you without incurring a penalty.

Before you sign on the dotted line

Make the local authority your first port of call when you start to look seriously for permanent premises. They will know what's available locally and what will best suit your needs. They are in daily contact with both the commercial and public sector property agents in your area. Talk to them, listen to them and take their advice before you sign on the dotted line. Watch out for business rates.

THE SYSTEMS YOU WILL NEED

Personal organisation

The best place to start is yourself. If *you're* organised it's a lot easier to organise everyone else around you. The essential tools you'll need won't cost much: an A4 pad and a pen. Last thing every night before you retire, list all the things you have to do the next day, then put them in order of priority with the nastiest piece of business right up there at the top. Crack that one first in the morning and the rest will disappear off your list in no time.

Treat every day in your new venture as an *ad*venture. To do that effectively, you must be personally very well organised.

Relevant and complementary systems

You'll need to devise and operate systems which complement your particular enterprise. There's nothing difficult about this but don't overdo the systems. Keep them relevant and simple. Whatever else, do concentrate on developing a system for effective debt collection suited to the nature of your business.

Using the help available

Browse through the business section of any major bookseller and you'll find a plethora of excellent and inexpensive paperbacks with tailormade systems and forms to cover the needs of almost any enterprise: accounting, distribution, sales, wages, tax, VAT, etc. Select the one that best suits your needs and adapt it accordingly.

Any other specific systems you may require will come to light along the way and you can devise them for yourself.

DECIDING YOUR BUSINESS STATUS

You have a choice of three possible routes with regard to the status of your enterprise. Your eventual choice will largely depend on the nature of the business.

Becoming a sole trader

There are certain initial financial advantages in operating as a sole trader but I would caution against it if you are looking for more substantial outside investment. Funders aren't too enthusiastic about lending to a one man or woman operation. Taxwise it is great for the first two years – but beware the new tax regulations for the self-employed.

The big disadvantage of the sole trader operation is that (God forbid) should it go down the pan you will be liable for all debts personally – unlimited liability, in fact.

Forming a partnership

In a partnership you and your partner legally share everything, the good and the bad. Your shares can be 50-50 or any other split you agree upon but always remember that once again you are faced with unlimited liability and you will each be responsible (separately and jointly) for all liabilities incurred in the name of the partnership.

Partnerships are obligatory in certain professional spheres, so again the nature of the business will determine whether this is the route to take. Otherwise do give it great consideration before deciding.

I would personally never enter into a partnership in business. Most partnership agreements are far too loosely defined and fraught with legal and financial hazards. Try getting out of one with your shirt intact when all goes wrong. To say it's not easy is an understatement.

Forming a limited company

This status will give you the most protection in all eventualities. Provided you act honestly and correctly, your personal liability is limited to the share capital you have invested in the company. Paradoxically you are likely to receive a friendlier ear when you go asking for external funding. But don't be fooled. You still have to give the banks belt-and-braces security against anything you borrow. Typically this will include having to give your personal guarantee for the company's overdraft or bank loans, and pledging personal assets such as a house in support of such guarantee.

As a limited company you'll also have a lot more clout with the public sector in the matter of grant and loan funding.

Think about it. Then ask your solicitor and accountant for professional advice.

UNDERSTANDING THE BASICS OF TAXATION

No matter how fulfilling you find running your own business, no matter how much money you make, you'll be simply chasing your tail and heading for trouble if you don't turn your attention to the basics of the taxation process:

- ☐ Income tax
- ☐ National Insurance contributions (NICs)
- ☐ Value Added Tax (VAT).

Who do you need to tell you've started a business?

As soon as you start up in business you must inform:

- ☐ your local tax office
- ☐ the Contributions Agency
- ☐ Customs & Excise (if your taxable turnover is to be in excess of £68,000 per annum, you must register for VAT).

What is income tax?

The main tax most people require to pay is income tax, which is charged on earnings of all kinds as well as on investment income such as bank interest. When you become self-employed or start up on your own in business you become responsible for paying your own tax and that is why you need to keep full and accurate records of all your business transactions.

Preparing your accounts

If you employ the services of an accountant, he will draw up your accounts. But whoever prepares them, you are still responsible for their accuracy and the correct declaration of the amount of profits.

Under Self Assessment, you are *not* required to send in your accounts with your tax return. Instead you will be requested to include the accounts information in a special section of the return. Your tax office may ask to see your accounts together with your business records to check against the figures in your completed return.

Simple tax returns

If your business turnover (total sales) before expenses is below £15,000 for a full year of trading, you will not have to provide detailed accounts information in the return. Instead, a simple three line summary will suffice. For example:

Turnover	£13,847
Less purchases and expenses	£ 3,017
Net profits	£10,830

Taxation for partnerships

Special rules apply for income tax purposes if you are in business with a partner. Basically your tax bill is calculated as if *your share* of the partnership is profits that you have made in business on your own.

What does 'Self Assessment' mean?

The Self Assessment system is intended to make individual tax matters clearer to people who regularly get tax returns. It is not a new tax.

What are National Insurance contributions?

These are five classes of contributions and the class you pay depends on whether you are an employee, self-employed, non-employed or an employer.

Self-employed persons are liable to pay two classes of contributions:

☐ Class 2 contributions

and

☐ Class 4 contributions, which are paid on profits and gains at or above a set level.

What is VAT?

VAT stands for 'Value Added Tax' and is a tax levied on most goods and services by the suppliers of those goods and services. Almost any business transaction can constitute what is known as a 'taxable supply' for VAT purposes, for example:

☐ sale of goods
☐ performance of services
☐ an exchange of goods or services
☐ a gift in kind.

Taxable supplies can be chargeable to VAT at the following rates:

☐ Zero rate: nil percentage applies
☐ Reduced rate: 5 per cent (limited to domestic fuel and power)
☐ Standard rate: 17.5 per cent (applied to all goods and services not exempt or liable at zero or reduced rates).

PREPARING TO SURVIVE – AND SUCCEED

Creating the right image

It's really important that you get this building block right, right from the start – so important that Chapter 6 examines the matter in detail. Remember, the image you will be creating for your business will be very largely influenced by the personal image you portray to the many and diverse personalities you will encounter in your day-to-day activities. Start working on a good personal image now. Get it right and you won't have to tinker with it later.

Surviving as a beginner

We are all beginners at the outset of any new enterprise. Indeed, this is no bad thing. Try hard not to surround yourself with 'experts' in your particular calling. Not only do they cost a lot of money, they are all too often set in their ways and unwilling to learn anything new.

I've always gone for brightness and enthusiasm before experience in the many new ventures I've been involved in over the years and never had cause to regret it.

Marketing your enterprise

People launching out on their own for the first time are often uneasy about the mechanics of marketing. They express concern about finding the correct application for their particular enterprise. Worry not. Chapter 6 will tell you in plain English what 'marketing' is and what it is definitely not. There's no mystique about it, only common sense.

Developing a sales strategy

Once you've developed your initial marketing strategy, you will find that the sales strategy for your business falls neatly into place. Start thinking about it now. Chapters 6 and 7 will lead you gently through the process of research to marketing to selling. Don't rush to them now though; read through the book in its entirety once, then go back to 5, 6 and 7 and study them again.

CASE STUDIES

Tom and Paula reach some key decisions

Tom meanwhile was pleased with his choice of partner. Paula had made substantial progress on developing the business plan and already they were discussing external funding, premises, business systems and the legal status their joint enterprise was to take.

As they were now both committed to the business they held their first (unofficial) board meeting and made decisions on the following:

1.   They would form a limited company.
2.   Tom would have 60 per cent of the equity, Paula 40 per cent.
3.   They would make early approaches to the public sector about possible grants and soft loan assistance.
4.   They set a date three months hence for the launch of the enterprise.
5.   Business would be initially conducted from Paula's home.
6.   Tom would start sourcing equipment.
7.   He would also start making appointments to visit his previous customers, advising them of the launch date.

Tom's dream was beginning to turn into a reality.

A bonus for Paul and Hazel

'Hey, I've just found our gravy wagon and I can get it for £350 less than you've budgeted for.'

'Paul, we don't want an old banger. We agreed.'

'But it's not a banger, it's in great nick. It belongs to Mr Pearson who's been on the same fast food route for years. He's retiring and what's more, we get his route thrown in for free. He says he doesn't want a cowboy moving in.'

'Fantastic, Paul. Now we just need to hear from "the Young People's Learning Agency" that our funding's OK and we're in business . . .'

John and Colin raise £5,000

John and Colin visited the local philanthropist at his home. Mr Watling had already studied the updated business plan which had been sent on to him in advance. He told them he was very interested in their project. He said he would like to invest some capital for which he did not require a return, only assurance that the money would be used solely as working capital. John and Colin received a cheque for £5,000.

ACTION POINTS

1. Draw up a brief outline of the accommodation you envisage your new enterprise will require for, say, an initial two year period. Will you really need premises for the first twelve months or so? Could you work from a room at home? Could you convert your garage?

2. Secondly, outline the basic systems you will need to begin with. Keep these systems simple and relevant and decide how best and cost-effectively you can implement them (purchasing, stock control, accounts, invoicing, cash collection, marketing, etc).

3. Look at the three options available to you in determining the legal status of your business. Which is best for you? What are the main implications of your final selection?

4. What kind of image do you want your business to reflect to others? Draw up an outline plan to achieve this.

5. What number and calibre of staff will you need at the outset? Work out job descriptions for each staff member.

6. Draw up a summary of your very first marketing strategy. From this plan devise the sales strategy for your business.

MARKETING YOUR ENTERPRISE

There is an incredible amount of rubbish talked about marketing. Much of it is based on little more than high-sounding jargon designed more to keep marketing pundits in business than to help business managers in the real world.

DEBUNKING THE MARKETING MYTH

Let's start with a basic definition of marketing:

- ☐ *Marketing is absolutely everything connected with the process by which a potential customer decides to buy (or not to buy).*

- ☐ Or, *marketing is communication.*

Communication is the essence of all business – and it's not necessarily the 'best talkers' who communicate best. You can communicate equally well by how you project your unique personality, how you articulate, how you relate to people without using words at all, how you listen to others.

What marketing is *not* is advertising, promotions, public relations, exhibitions, premiums, grand openings, closing down sales and the like – at least, not on their own individually or even collectively. It certainly includes all of these but a great deal more besides.

Marketing means a common sense approach to conducting your business. It starts and ends with *you*: how you dress, how you speak, how you approach your customers, how you treat your staff, how you set up your stall, in short, what kind of image you create for yourself and your enterprise.

It also has a lot to do with effective systems: how to react to problems, what kind of letters you send out, how to go about getting the cash in.

Let's examine a few of these essential aspects of pure marketing in the order of importance in which I would place them.

CREATING THE RIGHT PERSONAL IMAGE

Here's where your marketing programme really starts: with *you*. When you go out selling, you'll be marketing something much more potent than your product or service: you'll be selling *you* and you'll never stop selling *you*. Even when you've got a dozen salesmen out hustling, they'll still be selling *you*. This is not to imply that you ought to start thinking about changing *you*. You couldn't even if you tried. What it means is you have to be aware of *you* all the time and everywhere. How you project, how you dress, how you speak, how you earn (not command) respect. You're *you*. You're unique. Make the most of *you*. Think of some outstanding winners such as Richard Branson (Virgin), Anita Roddick (Bodyshop), or Victor Kiam (Remington).

The image your business will reflect

Customers, suppliers and staff will all develop an image of your new business in direct line with the image you project of yourself. They will see the business exactly according to the way you project it to them.

Millions of pounds are wasted annually by thousands of established companies in a vain attempt to improve their image. The problem frequently lies at the top, but has been around for so long that no one can see it for the fudge. That's how PR consultancies get rich. Make sure *you* get it right from the start.

Developing good customer relations

Clearly, if you don't get this right from the outset, you won't be around long enough to worry about the remainder of your marketing programme. But it's amazing how many start-ups make heavy weather of what is essentially a basic issue of dealing properly with other human beings – simple things, like correspondence, facing up to problems, cash collection, and the like. Every letter you send out should be an ambassador for your company: if you're unsure about the right style and format for a tricky situation, call on some help (there are several useful books on the market detailing suitable replies to almost every scenario you're likely to come across).

When faced with problems, address them immediately they come to light. You may not agree with the customer's point of view on all occasions but you must respect his right to express it. Try always to employ the 'win-win' formula, leaving the customer his dignity.

The right way to collect the cash

Getting the cash in on time is vital to every enterprise but most particularly so for the start-up. Never be afraid to ask for what you are due, when it is due. But do yourself a favour: be explicit from the start as to *exactly* what your payment terms are. Go on reminding your customers on every invoice and every statement you send out.

All the other good things you are doing will go for nought if you fail to get the cash in on time, every time. It's all to do with conditioning. To get your invoices nearer the top of the pile each month, condition your customers accordingly and keep on conditioning them. They won't tell you to shove off. They'll privately respect you for your principles (grudgingly perhaps, but that's OK).

Developing good staff relations

Even if your entire staff consists of just one other, there are two things you must accomplish without delay:

☐ Earn the respect of your staff through evidence of your own commitment.

☐ Instill in your staff your own personal philosophy of the business.

It sounds obvious, doesn't it? – So obvious in fact that most start-ups tend to ignore these two factors, imagining perhaps that respect should be automatic and that staff don't need to concern themselves with the philosophy behind the enterprise.

This is quite wrong. The best way to build your business in the early days is from within. Breed loyalty through involvement and you create a lasting team.

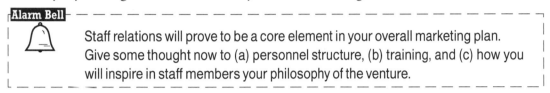

Alarm Bell

Staff relations will prove to be a core element in your overall marketing plan. Give some thought now to (a) personnel structure, (b) training, and (c) how you will inspire in staff members your philosophy of the venture.

Now we can progress to what most people consider to be 'marketing' but believe me, unless you are prepared to develop the right personal and business image, customer and staff relations, what you are about to read isn't worth a light.

Managing your promotional activities

This will sound like heresy coming from someone who spent 30 years at the top of the communications industry, but

☐ **Don't rush out and hire an advertising agency, a marketing specialist or a public relations consultancy.**

— Even if you reckon you need one of these, don't do it.
— Even if you've budgeted for it, don't do it.
— Even if the funders recommend it, don't do it.

Why not?

☐ **Because for the first 12 months you'll be far too busy developing your own personal image for *your* enterprise and the last thing you'll need is for some specialist who hasn't a clue about what makes you tick to create a false or artificial image for you which may turn out to be a Frankenstein monster that will devour you.**

If after a year you think the business warrants it, then go out and hire all three if you like, but not before.

So what sort of promotional activity are you going to undertake during your initial year of trading? In short, not a lot and only that which is absolutely necessary and which you can afford. By not a lot, I mean not a lot that costs you money but there's a great deal of useful work you can do for next to nothing.

Building up your image

This is the very first thing you give your attention to and here's where I advise you spend a *little* money to ensure that it's right, right from the start. We are all of us gifted with at least some personal creativity. When I reviewed a series of personally produced logos for my own company I thought one of them was absolutely brilliant. But when I took a step back, I began to realise that not only was it naff, it was also unworkable because of technical reproduction reasons (and the logo was produced by a trained designer).

Call in some objective, unbiased professional help: not a high priced design consultancy. There are lots of bright proficient young people out there with Apple Macs who will do you a superb job at the right price. Just explain in your own words what you're all about, and let them come up with proposals. Make sure, too, that you don't cheesepare on your stationery. Choose good quality paper and printing.

Get the 'front of the house' right too. Even if your reception area is the size of a broom closet, invest a little money to create an ambience where you can portray your business with a touch of class.

Creating your first brochure

You're going to require some modest piece of print matter to explain your enterprise and why prospective customers or clients should consider using you. Again this will cost a little money, but not too much if you go about its production in the right way.

First off, write down some notes about your initial customer base. Then go back and chat to your friendly young designer, and get him/her to produce a rough outline in tandem with the image already created. Ask him/her to call in a 'tame' printer (they will all know several who are as hungry as they are) and get a detailed written quote for printing the number you require. You won't be disappointed in the price.

There's something in it for both of them. It's called networking: the development of business through a growing network of contacts working with each other. Then, when your brochure has been produced (and if you've been successful in obtaining a marketing support grant) send a copy of it together with copies of all the relevant invoices to your local Skills Funding Agency and you could well get a rebate of 30 to 50 per cent. That's networking, too.

MARKETING RESEARCH

Here we will see how your business can be helped by 'marketing' research (as distinct from 'market' research). You'll want to be thinking about extending your limited promotional activity into other areas of your market. These areas are already well defined but you may have no idea how to approach them or whom to approach. This is a very common situation for start-up concerns and one best tackled as quickly as possible. It is also an area where you can do yourself a lot of good at minimal expense. Let's take for example the launch of my own enterprise.

Example

The business of my company is specialist publishing, exclusively for local authorities throughout the United Kingdom. The patch I really knew (including competitor activity) was Scotland and the North East of England. The remainder of the UK market was well defined through trade directories, but what I didn't know was which officer had the responsibility for which of several relevant publications in which region, county, borough or district. Before pressing the print button on my company brochure I needed to establish actual *contact* points for the entire market. But how?

Easy! I went straight to the top. I penned a carefully worded letter accompanied by a simple questionnaire and prepaid reply envelope to every Chief Executive in every region, county, borough and district in the United Kingdom. The letter didn't mention it came from a business start-up but simply asked for help in updating current intelligence on publishing contact points within the local authority.

A dramatic response

The response factor was dramatic. Out of 800-odd requests, I received 523 impeccably completed responses. This yielded a potential customer database of 1,400 names to whom I mailed out personalised letters (plus brochure). From this exercise I derived excellent conversion ratios: over 100 qualified requests for appointments over a period of time and subsequently confirmed contracts worth a great deal of money. Even more importantly, the exercise resulted in a valuable database which could be refined before impending UK local government reorganisation – a situation where current intelligence was critical.

You, too, can achieve things at very little cost when you start out. Just look at your market, decide what you need to know, then find a way to get the information you require by simply *asking* for it.

ABOVE THE LINE PROMOTION

Above the line promotion means the kinds of promotion you buy in, for example to get a message across – for example advertising, PR and exhibitions. Let's consider them one by one.

Advertising

'Advertising' can have a very narrow, or very wide, meaning. It can easily mean expending an inordinate amount of money on exposure by sundry media activity: press, television, radio, hoardings and the like. For your first 12 months in business, you may well not need it. You will need to find some way of checking how much business (and profits) you actually achieve for each £100 of expenditure. If you don't budget sensibly, participation will cost you dearly and could bleed you dry.

Public or press relations

Nowadays to the cognoscenti this is often simply 'Relations'. Whatever, this is where you can really do yourself some good at next to no cost. Here's how:

☐ Identify the trade journals relevant to your enterprise and establish the editorial contacts for your area. Do the same with your local press media (including free sheets). The cost of a few telephone calls will elicit this information.

☐ Now make it your business to cultivate these new found contacts. Send a short press release to all of them about the launch of your enterprise and follow up this activity with personal introductions by telephone. Your strike rate first time around probably won't be very high but the important thing you will have achieved is contact.

☐ Keep up the good work with regular calls and releases on orders attained, new staff appointments and any other good news you can think of. These press contacts are going to be very useful to you for a long time to come.

The media are always on the lookout for news and if you continue to service them well, they'll eventually start coming to you as an authority for views on issues which relate specifically to your industry. All of this you can do for yourself without recourse to big ticket consultancies. It can also be a lot of fun.

Exhibitions

Depending on the nature of your business, public or trade exhibitions can be a great source of opportunity for the start-up. However, they can be quite costly and outside the range of most emergent concerns. If, on the other hand, you have a public sector marketing grant upon which to draw, and you know of a local exhibition which would help you, then do consider taking a small stand during your first year of trading. It can be a superb way of accelerating a company's database of prospective customers.

☐ Do you plan to advertise during the first year?
☐ Who will handle press and public relations for your business?
☐ Will you participate in local exhibitions?

Times of recession can colour your marketing plans. Email *jimgreen@writing-for-profit.com* with RECESSION in the subject line and I'll send you a useful PDF handbook to help you through the worst times.

AVOIDING MISTAKES IN SMALL BUSINESS MARKETING

How do you judge the effectiveness of your small business marketing efforts? Easy … does it produce results? Great looking ads, fancy logos and flashy websites are worthless if they don't bring business to your door. This list of 10 common marketing mistakes can help you produce better results.

Not having a clearly defined USP

Do you want to fit in or stand out? In order to thrive in today's cluttered marketplace, every small business owner must be able to clearly articulate an answer to the question, 'Why should someone do business with you rather than your competitor?' What makes you unique? Your answer to these questions constitutes your Unique Selling Proposition (USP). Do you offer 24-hour, 7-day a week service? Do you offer the lowest price? Do you offer a no-risk guarantee? A strong USP helps you to stand out in a crowded field.

Selling features rather than benefits

Someone once said, 'No one ever bought a drill bit. Millions of people have bought a hole'. People don't buy features, they buy benefits. They are tuned into Radio Station W.I.I.F.M. (What's in it for me?) Tell them clearly how the features of your product/service will help them make their life easier, etc.

Not using headlines in print advertisements

You have at most a couple of seconds to grab someone's attention when they read a newspaper, magazine, etc. Using an attention-grabbing headline ensures that the reader will continue to read the rest of the advertisement. The headline is an ad for the ad. Take a look at some newspaper ads. Which ones attract your attention? You will probably find they have utilised an effective headline.

Not testing headlines, price points, packages, pitches, everything

How do you know what ad, what price, what offer most appeals to customers? By putting them to a vote. Test everything. Rather than running one newspaper ad for three weeks, why not run three different ads for three weeks and measure which draws better? Rather than putting all your advertising into newspapers, why not split it between newspaper and direct mail and measure the results? Why not price your products/services at different points and see which sells more? Is cheaper always better? Not necessarily. Each situation is unique. One price may outperform another for a myriad of reasons. Your job is not to know why, but to find what works. Test, test, test.

Making it difficult to do business with you

Is your sales staff knowledgeable about your products? Does someone answer your phone promptly and in a friendly manner? Can people find your phone number, location? Can customers find things easily in your store? Put yourselves in your customer's shoes. Don't make them work – because they won't. I've seen a website that undoubtedly cost the company thousands of pounds and **nowhere** could I find a phone number or email address. Your customer has better things to do than struggle to do business with you.

Not finding out what your customer's needs are

What is the first step in filling your customer's needs? Discovering what they are. What's most important to them? Don't even try to guess. You may think price is most important when what they really want is fast service. You may believe fast service is what they want when what they desperately want is a friendly, personal touch. How do you find out? People won't tell you unless you ask. So ask.

Not maintaining an up-to-date customer database

Your customer list is pure gold. Rather than always working to bring new customers in the door, why not take advantage of the goodwill you have already built with your existing clientele? Experiment with extending special offers to your customer base. Ask for referrals. Send them a card on their birthday. Call and ask what they most enjoyed about doing business with you (or what they disliked about doing business with you). You work hard to develop these relationships. Recognise their value and work hard to 're-delight' them.

Not eliminating the risk

What stops a customer from buying from you? Are they unsure that your offer is worth their hard-earned money? Make it easy to decide to buy from you. How can you reduce their risk? If you are in a service business, let them try your service at no cost. If you are a lawyer or consultant offer them a free consultation. Offer them a money back, no questions asked guarantee on any product they buy. Why not? Are you afraid people will take advantage of you? Give it a try for a month. You may be very pleasantly surprised. Not confident in your product or service? Then go to work on improving your service.

Not educating your customers

Don't just claim that your service is better. Explain why. Is your staff better trained? Do you utilise a technology that increases service turnaround or quality? Don't expect people to just take your word for things. Quality, service and value mean nothing. Everyone claims to offer these. Make these claims real for the customer by offering credible explanations why they should do business with you.

Not knowing what works, and sticking with it

Do you know which ads are effective? What media pulls best? What offer gets the best reaction? By testing (see above) you will. When you find something that works, don't change it until you find something that works better. Just because you're sick of an ad/offer isn't a good enough reason to change it. You can supplement with other ads and offers. If it works, keep it.

CASE STUDIES

Tom and Paula plan their strategy

The initial marketing strategy for Tom and Paula's new enterprise is now well advanced. The entrepreneurial training programme has given both of them an insight into what marketing is really all about.

Conscious of his lack of experience in face-to-face selling, Tom has enrolled in a short government sponsored course on the science of selling. Meantime, Paula is devoting her energies to working out the overall marketing strategy, providing detailed guidelines on responsibilities for each of them.

Tom and Paula have decided that for the first year of operation their promotional activity will be restricted to producing a suitable brochure, and sharing a small stand at a local exhibition for the printing trade.

Paul and Hazel shop around

Hazel received a telephone call from The Young People's Learning Agency requesting another meeting with both of them. The executive explained that she had been successful in obtaining a grant for them of £1,000 from a charitable trust who specialised in supporting innovative self-employment projects wholly devised and enacted by young unemployed persons. The remaining £500 would come to them by way of a soft loan from the public sector.

When they got back home Paul secured the mobile van with a deposit and Hazel shopped around for a discount on a microwave oven.

Our young entrepreneurs were in business and it hadn't taken half as long as they had first thought.

'See, I told you we could do it.'

'Okay bighead. Sorry . . . Boss.'

Donation launches the business

With Mr Watling's generous donation to the 'Comely Coaches' venture, John and Colin were also in business. After another meeting with all the parties concerned, the contract with Social Services was signed. The community services project dreamed up on the bowling green was underway.

ACTION POINTS

1. Describe the essence of 'marketing'.

2. Show how you would set about developing a personal image for your enterprise.

3. List ways of acquiring cost-free publicity for your new business.

4. Draw up a Customer Charter for your enterprise, stating how you will greet them, how regularly you will call on them, how you will handle complaints, etc.

5. Draw up a similar charter for staff relations.

6. Jot down the most important things you don't yet know about your market. Devise a simple plan for essential marketing research. Then make a plan for your very first promotional campaign.

7

CULTIVATING THE SELLING HABIT

You've produced a winning plan, you've got all your funding in position, your image is looking good, your brand new stationery still has the smell of printer's ink and perhaps you've moved into bright new premises already.

HOW TO BEGIN

☐ *You start from Day One developing the selling habit, and you keep on improving your sales sense until the day you retire or sell out.*

Even if you find it hard to acquire the selling habit to start with, after a while you'll discover that it is a very difficult habit to give up.

All you've been doing so far is setting up your stall and now you're about to embark on the biggest learning curve of your life. Even if you've been in sales for the whole of your career, you'll still be starting at square one because this time it's *all* down to you.

But what if your career path has been in a different direction altogether? What if you've never sold face-to-face before? How are you going to master the art in a short space of time?

The fact is that – whether you realise it or not – you've been selling face-to-face since the day you were born.

☐ Every time you negotiated for extra pocket money, you were selling.
☐ Every time you asked the boss for a salary increase, you were selling.
☐ Every time you talked your way out of trouble, you were selling.

LEARNING TO NEGOTIATE

☐ *What to remember when you're out there hustling is that you cannot actually SELL anything to anybody. They'll BUY from you, but only if they identify with* **you.**

That's precisely why getting *your* image right, right from the start, is the most crucial piece of marketing activity you'll ever undertake.

A formula to help you

But there must be some kind of formula for successfully developing the selling habit? There is. It's simplicity itself and it is adaptable to any situation. Let's examine this formula piece by piece, and then create a face-to-face scenario in the office of a potential customer whom you've never met before.

The selling formula

1. Prospect for your customers.
2. Make your appointments.
3. Clinch your deals face-to-face.

PROSPECTING FOR CUSTOMERS

As with all things in life, you must have a plan if you are to succeed. In this scenario, you want to provide yourself with a steady stream of prospects to buy advertising space in the range of local authority publications you will be handling. Here's your plan:

1. If the publication you have been assigned to is a 'repeat' (a second or third edition) then every advertiser in these editions is a prospect.

2. If it's a new publication, then any other recent handbook sponsored by the council will contain lots of prospects. It's a matter of simple common sense to determine those which are of particular relevance to your project – but consider them *all* as potential customers. Advertisers buy into these publications for all sorts of reasons which are not always obvious.

3. Look through the sponsored publications circulating in your catchment area. You'll see certain advertisers appearing again and again, even though there would seem to be no common link between the publications. These advertisers have multiple reasons for buying. Add them to your list.

4. Council supplier lists are an excellent source for prospects. Very often you'll pick up sales from these suppliers for 'emotional' reasons, *ie* they are currently doing business with the council – or would like to.

5. Local newspapers, free sheets and *Yellow Pages* are also full of suitable prospects. Refer to them regularly.

6. If you are working out of a local authority office, cultivate your temporary colleagues. The book you are working on is very close to their hearts and they'll gladly help you in any way they can to provide you with potential customers.

7. Drive around the local trading estates and jot down the names of companies who fit the profile of your book. Add them to your list.

☐ *Apply yourself diligently to these seven steps each day and you'll rapidly build a database that will amaze you.*

Alarm Bell

Do this exercise now. Create an outline plan for prospecting based on the specific requirements of the niche in which you intend to operate. Review your jottings and then rearrange them in chronological order.

MAKING YOUR APPOINTMENTS

A golden rule

You always use the telephone to 'sell the appointment' – not to make the sale! This is the cardinal error committed time and time again by the eager beavers going nowhere fast in the business of professional selling. Ours is a considered sale where the appointment is vital. We can then effectively demonstrate the product, sell the benefits, and clinch the sale.

Example

Hot prospects

From your accumulated prospects list, pick out enough 'hot ones' (say 30) to provide a pattern for your first week's appointments.

Territory management

Use the technique of 'territory management': arrange these in such a way that you could comfortably visit six per day (three morning, three afternoon) without risking a nervous breakdown.

Allocating times

Now make out lists for each day for these 'manageable' visits. Against each prospect allocate an appointment time (9.30, 10.30, 11.30, *etc*).

You now have an ideal appointments pattern for the week ahead. 'But how I can possibly expect prospects to conveniently fit in with my schedule?' If you have such a plan prepared *before* you make your telephone calls, you'll be pleasantly surprised how many people do fit in. Sure, you'll have to make the odd adjustment now and again but nothing like as drastically as you would without a plan. Try it. It works.

Your calls record

Now take a sheet of plain A4 paper and rule it exactly as the specimen sheet on page 66. This is your 'Calls Record'. Don't be fooled into thinking that this is pedantic or unnecessary. It's not. You need to keep an accurate record of your calls to determine what your strike rate is in:

☐ getting through to prospects
☐ clinching appointments.

By filling in the 'Calls Record' as you telephone, you will find that your confidence grows and your strike rate gradually improves.

'D'=DIALS.   You may have to dial several times before being connected. Log the dials.

'C' =CALLS.   Your initial call may have only connected you to the switchboard. Your prospect may be out or at a meeting. Log the calls.

'CC'=CONFIRMED CALLS. You've made it through to the prospect. Log the confirmed calls.

Totting up these entries at the end of your call sessions gives you an assessment of your improving performance.

Now you're ready to make those calls

You've done your homework, you've got your 'Calls Record' in front of you and now you're ready to make those calls in a confident and relaxed frame of mind.

All you need now is a draft script (**cue sheet**) to help you take charge of all your calls. You don't have to stick rigidly to it. In fact, it works better if you vary it according to how you instinctively relate to each individual prospect. Remember, no two people are alike, or react in the same way.

The cue sheet places you firmly in the driver's seat at the beginning of each conversation. Here's an example of the kind of cue sheet we use at Focus Publishing. It works well for us and you can easily adapt it to your own needs.

A scripted call

'Good morning, my name is Jim Green of Focus Publishing. We haven't met before but I was given your name as someone who might be interested in having their company included in the new edition of the Business Directory which Focus is currently compiling for X County Council. I'd like to make an appointment to come and see you. Would 10am tomorrow suit you? I promise not to take up much of your time – 15 minutes should do it.'

All this has taken no more than 30 seconds of relaxed delivery and already the prospect in question has been informed of:

- ☐ the caller's name
- ☐ the caller's company
- ☐ what the caller wants from the prospect (*ie* a brief appointment)
- ☐ when the caller *ideally* wants the appointment.

At this point any of the following can happen:

1.   If the prospect's intrigued he'll agree to see the caller at the *caller's* appointed time.

2.   If the date/time doesn't suit, he'll either suggest an alternative or ask the caller for one.

3.   He may claim he's too busy to see the caller and ask for details by post or fax. The caller should desist from accepting this alternative, intimating that the proposition requires a brief personal meeting to do it justice.

DATE	PROSPECT	D	C	CC	REMARKS
Mon 6 May	Fyfe Cement	1	2	1	* 10am Tues 7th
	MDC Windows	3	2	1	* 3pm Wed 8th
	Greyshom Dev.	1	1	1	Call back
	Campbell Const.	1	1	–	Closed for hols.
	Scotwest Plumbers	2	2	1	* 11am Wed 8th
	Midscot Training	1	1	1	Call back Thurs
	Shanks Printers	1	1	1	* 11am Thurs 9th
	Pioneer Builders	3	1	–	No response
	Tilcon Mortars	4	3	1	* 12.30 Fri first
	Loudon Plastics	4	2	–	Can't reach . . .
	Sullivan Signs	6	4	1	* 3pm Fri (will sign)
	Patterson Sols.	2	1	1	Not interested
	Thern Enterprise	2	1	1	* 2pm today (will sign)
	Tack Development	3	1	1	* 3pm today (will sign)
	Davidson Arch.	2	1	1	Call back Thurs.
	Dyke Workshops	4	1	1	Unavailable. Call back
	Bonnar & Co	3	2	1	Not interested
		43	27	14	* 8 appointments

CONVERSATION RATIOS FOR ONE DAY'S TELEPHONE ACTIVITY

CALLS	63%
CONFIRMED CALLS	33%
APPPOINTMENTS	19%

(i.e. 27 calls/43 dials x 100 = 63%)

Fig. 3. Example of 'calls records'.

4.   The prospect may say 'get lost'. Depending upon his mettle, the caller can either accept that or try to convince the prospect that he's missing out on a good thing by refusing an appointment. (A good plan here is to hint that a competitor has already signed up.)

☐ Remember – what you're selling when you telephone is an appointment not the product or service. That comes later when you meet the prospect face-to-face.

CLINCHING A DEAL FACE-TO-FACE

Now you're here at the point of sale and there's no more exciting place to be for the committed professional. You've done your homework and secured an appointment. What's more, you've already gleaned some knowledge about your prospect's business, what it does and how it markets its product. Now you are going to impress the prospect with your knowledge.

In-and-out with a sale in 15 minutes

You're going to be in-and-out with an order in just 15 minutes and here's how you're going to do it:

1.   Thank the prospect for agreeing to meet you and briefly (very briefly) introduce yourself and the company.

2.   Describe the nature of your product or service and say how it will **benefit** the marketing of the prospect's enterprise.

3.   Produce a sample of your product (or a fact sheet/brochure if it's a service). Explain in a little detail why it's so special, where it scores over the competition and how your prospect would benefit from doing business with you.

4.   While you're doing this, handle your sample (or brochure) with tender care as if it were some precious stone. Then hand it to the prospect to touch, examine, browse through as the case may be. Watch out for **buying signals**.

5.   Diplomatically answer any **objections** the prospect may raise.

6.   ASK FOR THE SALE.

7.   Complete the order, get it signed . . . and leave.

Asking for the sale

Let's look again at 6 and 7 in more detail:

Ask for the sale

This is where
the eager beavers
invariably

fall down...
It's simple.
Just **ask** for it
and if your presentation is good
you'll probably get it.
If not,
ask for it again.

This time
you'll get it.

Don't hang about
...and when you do
get your order...
complete the details
swiftly but *accurately*,
thank your prospect for his business,
refuse a cup of coffee
and **leave**.

Hang about and you'll risk
talking yourself
out of the sale
in a fraction of the time
it took you
to make it.

Where the eager beavers fall down

The eager beavers ignore the essential rules of negotiation:

- □ they're too keen (and it shows)
- □ they talk too much (unsettling the prospect)
- □ they ignore buying signals (they can't see them)
- □ they gloss over the benefits (going for an early kill)
- □ they make mistakes in their presentation (talking too much).

Don't be an eager beaver. Adopt the laid back, listening approach. Give the prospect a chance to talk, encourage him to talk. He'll tell you all about *his business*. He'll just love telling you about his business and then when you leave with your order, he'll tell everyone what a wonderful conversationalist you are. That's selling.

Avoid the rinky-dink sales approach

The rinky-dink is the 'no problem' merchant who causes no end of trouble for everyone else in the organisation. He will promise *anything* to land a sale and in the process lands himself in the drink. You can't afford to be like this. In the early days of your enterprise there will be no one else around to bail you out if you promise what you can't deliver.

Asking for 'yes' when they keep saying 'no'

You must always be prepared for a 'no'. Be philosophical about receiving 'no' for an answer and steely enough to go back again and again to convert a 'no' into a 'yes'. When you start out you'll have no track record, and will be looking for people to take you on trust. Don't let that put you off. 'No' doesn't necessarily mean 'no', as we'll discuss in Chapter 10.

Stripping away the mystique of sales

There's no mystique about selling. It's simply a matter of cultivating the science of negotiation, ensuring that every deal is done on the win-win basis: not just something for you, but something for the prospect as well.

THE TEN COMMANDMENTS OF SELLING

1. **Never fail to turn up for an appointment**
   If it's impossible to make it, telephone in advance advising the prospect why you can't be there on time.

2. **Never promise anything you can't deliver**
   If you do, you'll lose your integrity.

3. **Never knock the competition**
   Don't even mention them, let the prospect do that.

4. **Never argue with a prospect**
   You'll lose out if you do.

5. **Never leave a lost sale thinking it's lost forever**
   The deal may not have been right for him now but it may be later.

6. **Never turn up for an appointment reeking of alcohol**
   You're dead if you do.

7. **Never deviate from the purpose of the meeting**
   The prospect doesn't want to know what a wonderful person you are.

8. **Never take rejection to heart**
   You won't appreciate your wins until you've suffered the odd loss.

9. **Never be afraid to admit you blew it**
   You'll only be deceiving yourself if you do.

10. **Never fail to keep your sales records up to date**
    If you don't you won't get paid on time.

Successful people all love selling. It's the lifeblood of any enterprise. Get your act together, go out there and sell, sell, sell.

 Seasoned professionals have one thing in common; they never stop learning new techniques on face-to-face selling. Here's a tip; visit this website *http://tinyurl.com/ygdqfjg* where you will find hosts of strategies and tools for start-ups.

TEN WAYS TO INCREASE YOUR SALES

Begin by differentiating your products or services by who you are and what your business is all about. What makes you different? Is it better training, experience, methodology, teamwork? Come up with your core advantages over the competition.

1. **If customers can buy a similar product/service for less**
   Be prepared to overcome that obstacle. Agree with them that they can buy for less but demonstrate that they may be comparing apples to oranges.

2. **Always sell based on perceived value**
   Describe exactly what benefits the customer will derive from purchasing your produce.

3. **Stress the quality of your proposition**
   Demonstrate how your produce quality outstrips that of the competition.

4. **Talk about dependability**
   Tell customers how long you've been in business, the breadth of your experience and commercial background. Then demonstrate the dependability of your produce/service by listing the benefits of purchase. Add to this any testimonials you have received from satisfied buyers.

5. **Show what separates you from others**
   Do you provide something that others don't? Do you have an edge on the competition on quality, service, ranges or whatever?

6. **Provide outstanding follow-up service**
   Frequently customers complain after a sale that there is no follow-up contact. Set yourself apart by providing personalised service irrespective of calls upon it.

7. **Offer a no-strings money back guarantee**
   Make prospects feel secure about buying from you. Tell them they can have a free trial with satisfaction guaranteed or money refunded without quibble. You'll cut down dramatically on refunds if you do.

8. **Accept credit cards even if your competitors don't**
   More and more people worldwide are becoming comfortable about using credit cards to conduct sales transactions. Cash in on the trend or lose out if you don't.

9. **Target a niche the competition doesn't reach**
Sell to prospects no one else bothers about and you'll capture a sub-sector of the market all for yourself.

10. **Never sell yourself short**
If your produce is superior to that of the competition price it accordingly and explain to prospects why it's worth more.

TEN WAYS TO CONVERT PROSPECTS INTO BUYERS

1. **Reduce fear by eliminating doubt**
Eliminate all traces of doubt in the minds of prospects and you will reduce the fear factor to nil. They will buy with confidence and present you with the opportunity of converting them into lifetime customers.

2. **Be gracious and caring as opposed to hungry and uncaring**
Never give the impression you need customers to survive. Potential buyers smell this come-on a mile off – and run.

3. **Focus on what the buyer finds interesting about your proposition**
Buyers don't care about product features. They're only interested in what benefits will accrue when they make a purchase. Stress benefits, not features.

4. **Ask the sort of questions that will help you understand the buyer's preferences**
Take an interest in what the prospect's really looking for. Don't be bashful. Ask meaningful questions – but don't turn into a machine gun.

5. **Become a walking example of the benefits of your produce**
Credibility will be instantly established when you learn how to effortlessly convey the superiority of your produce. Your power of gentle persuasion will transfer itself from you to the product or service.

6. **How to help impulse buyers to an experience they haven't enjoyed before**
Many people are tempted to buy on emotion, validate the facts when they return home, and frequently come back looking for a refund. Enlighten the impulse buyer with product information and heighten the impulse to make a firm decision to purchase.

7. **Don't forget to mention what the product *won't* do**
Never allow a prospect to make a purchase thinking the product will do something for them that it won't. Highlight, stress and be excited about your produce but always be truthful about its limitations.

8. **Make prospects feel they are important to you**
Why? Because they are; contented prospects convert into satisfied customers.

9. **Ensure that the prospect knows you believe in your produce**
If you cannot demonstrate conviction no one else will.

10. **Don't cold call – get referrals**

If you are not being referred to others by your clientele then you are not doing as good a job for them as you think. Work on it – it's fixable.

CASE STUDIES

Tom and Paula agree their sales policy

The marketing strategy has produced an agreed sales policy for the business and Tom and Paula have decided on the following:

1. The initial market will consist of Tom's previous contacts whom he has been calling on regularly and from several of whom he has had requests for quotations.

2. The focus will be on pricing: not discounting but more of a value-for-money policy without impairing margins.

3. Paula will concentrate on new business development as an on-going project using telemarketing techniques from her home base.

Tom's course on the science of selling is already beginning to pay dividends. He feels much more confident in one-to-one situations.

Hazel's brainwave

'We'll have to think about some marketing, Paul. To get us up and running.'

'You what?'

'Marketing. Well, some leaflets then, I suppose. It's all we can afford.'

'Who are we going to hand them out to?'

'I've thought about that. School playgrounds for a start. Kids are always hungry. Remember how we used to be?'

'That chap at the Young People's Learning Agency. He said he could help us with leaflets.'

'Then let's call him, Paul.'

ACTION POINTS

1. Describe in detail how you will prepare for customer prospecting, making appointments and clinching the deals face-to-face.

2. Construct a script you'll feel personally comfortable with for face-to-face selling.

8
DEVELOPING THE RIGHT QUALITIES

Entrepreneurship calls for a strange, sometimes conflicting mixture of qualities but they are all essential in one way or another. The reason you must develop these qualities is so you can automatically shift up or down a gear as you face ever changing circumstances. This way you will always be in control.

SEVENTEEN ESSENTIAL QUALITIES

Place a tick beside those qualities you possess.

1. ambition   _____

2. persistence   _____

3. endurance   _____

4. obduracy   _____

5. understanding   _____

6. empathy   _____

7. articulation   _____

8. confidence   _____

9. decisiveness   _____

10. humour   _____

11. persuasion   _____

12. intuition   _____

13. temperance   _____

14. patience   _____

15. style   _____

16. service   _____

17. humility   _____

DISCOVERING AMBITION

Ambition

Unless you're chock full of this, you'll be sunk before you start. How high is your ambition? Do you want to be a millionaire in five years' time? Perhaps the accumulation of wealth is unimportant to you, and your ambition takes other forms – status, personal development, security, recognition by others.

The really important thing to establish before you set out on your journey is the extent of your ambition and in which direction it lies. Establish that early on and you can devote all your energies to achieving what you *really* want from your endeavours.

That's the critical mistake I made first time round. I didn't truly know where I wanted my ambition to lead me and as a result I paid a heavy penalty.

QUALITIES TO ADD STEELINESS

Persistence

Once you are clear where you want to get to, be prepared to persist until you achieve all of your goals. There is no point in putting so much work and effort into a plan if you fail to carry it out.

The real achievers in life are not necessarily captains of industry or high profile personalities; they are those ordinary people who go about their business quietly and persistently, ticking off each goal as it is achieved.

Your plans won't just fall into line, because things don't just 'happen'. You have to make them happen through persistent effort.

Endurance

Definition: n. 'power of enduring; bearing (hardship) patiently'. Notice the word in parentheses. It's optional. Obstacles only become hardships when you allow them to. Much better to exercise your power and endure the obstacles you will encounter along the way until you find a way to turn them around into victories.

There's an old song which contains a famous line:

> There's no one with endurance like the man who sells insurance

… and there are many successful entrepreneurs in the insurance industry.

Obduracy

This is not a very desirable quality but you'll need a smidgeon of it in your make-up. There are times when you'll have to be really stubborn to get things done. Only be obdurate when you know for sure that what you believe is indeed the right thing.

You must also expect to be seen as hardhearted at times, as when you have to fire someone because they are fouling up the operation. People don't always see it your way.

RELATING WELL TO PEOPLE

Understanding

Expect to be asked for a great deal of understanding on your way to the top. People will expect it of you: understanding why the goods didn't arrive on schedule, understanding why customers can't pay you for another month, understanding why three members of the staff are all going on holiday at the same time – understanding all manner of things.

Whatever, don't lose your cool. The answer often lies in communication, or the lack of it. Listen carefully to what everyone has to say, then take your own counsel in resolving the situation. That doesn't mean steam-rolling. It means negotiating for a win-win result.

Showing empathy

Empathy goes a little deeper than simple understanding. It means developing the power to enter into and understand another's feelings without intrusion. True empathy takes a lot of patient practice but it will pay you handsomely if you perfect your technique. Never try it as a subterfuge, though; it will certainly backfire.

To exercise empathy you must be totally honest with yourself and the other person involved.

Being articulate

This does not mean talking like a BBC Radio 3 announcer with a plum in his mouth. It simply means expressing your thoughts very clearly in your own words, in your own accent, but in such a way that everyone can understand you. If you can do this efficiently all the time, you'll find it very helpful if called upon to engage in public speaking.

Displaying confidence

Confidence is a quality all entrepreneurs have or acquire, but not always in a way you'd notice. More often than not their confidence manifests itself as quiet self-assurance which seems to inspire confidence in others.

Example

Take Richard Branson for example: nice young chap who apparently doesn't have a suit to his name yet controls multi-million pound empires casually (seemingly) with a unique laid-back approach to commerce. He's got all the confidence in the world and a genuine smile always at the ready to go with it.

Being enthusiastic

You'll have noticed that Richard Branson is also brimming with this quality, too. They go hand in hand: confidence and enthusiasm. You can't have one without the other. Even when your stomach is turning over and you feel the pits, you have to keep your enthusiasm boiling over. It's infectious, keeps others on their toes and will keep you at the top of the heap.

Being decisive

The entrepreneur never has a problem making a decision in any situation where a clear decision is called for. Because of his experience in looking problematic situations straight in the face, the entrepreneur can weigh up the pros and cons very rapidly and just as quickly come to a reasoned decision. The entrepreneur will stick by that decision when others around are expressing doubts.

Acting speedily

Akin to decisiveness is speed of action in every undertaking. You've heard the old adage, 'If you want something done in a hurry, ask a busy man.' This is not to imply that you should rush through your everyday tasks like there was no tomorrow. On the contrary, do all you have to do each day but do it in your own time on a wholly organised basis. This way you will prioritise your activities, perform them all efficiently, recognise instantly when something requires immediate attention and generally get yourself up to entrepreneurial speed calmly and effortlessly.

The need for humour

You'll need a pretty good sense of humour for the road ahead, which you will find is so often full of Dismal Johnnies. A well developed sense of humour will lift you well clear of so many emotional traps.

Persuasiveness

This is a very handy quality to have. You'll never (without employing undue pressure) get anyone to do anything they really don't want to do, but with gentle persuasion you can often get people to see things your way if they're hovering on the brink.

Example

Suppose you're selling cars. Tell the customer who wants the best part exchange terms that his car is exactly what you've been looking for, is in great nick for its year and is a credit to its owner. In short, make it clear that you're really pleased he came along. As a skilled business person you should have a bit of margin to play around with in the mark-up of the car you're trying to persuade him to buy.

Using your intuition

Intuition is a magnificent quality if you know how to use it properly. Call it what you will – intuition, creative thinking, inspiration, lateral thinking. You can't buy it, you can't rent it, but you can certainly develop it.

Good intuition is a matter of listening to and cultivating the inner voice. It's best accomplished when you're relaxing, your mind is unburdened and you have left the cares of the day behind. Try, it really works.

Remaining temperate

Keeping calm, and keeping a sense of proportion, are not always easy for those of us with a compulsive nature, but it's a quality it will pay you to develop in business. Being temperate means keeping moderation in all things, for example treating adversity with same equanimity as success.

Being patient

Whether you like it or not, you will need a great deal of patience if you are to be a successful entrepreneur – patience with your staff, patience with customers, patience with suppliers, patience as you wait for a result, patience in everything you undertake.

Developing your own style

You'll want bags of style as you promote your image as a budding entrepreneur. Develop style in how you dress, style in how you talk, style in how you walk and lots of style in handling sticky situations.

Learning to give good service

Of all the qualities listed in this chapter, giving good service to others is the catalyst which sparks off all the other qualities. All great men and women in history have exemplified the quality of service often without thought of reward. As someone in business, you are being *paid* to provide good service to others, so make sure you really do from day one.

Every day we all see endless examples of rotten service. Most of us simply put up with it because we think that's the way of the world. It's not. The business person who makes service to others a top priority will progress by leaps and bounds and leave the competition standing.

Example

The day before I completed this chapter I was having breakfast in a hotel in Worcester and had to ask three times before I got the pot of coffee I'd ordered some time earlier. The general level of service in that hotel wouldn't have passed muster in a shanty town in Nebraska let alone New York City. In the end, the patrons will simply spend their money elsewhere.

Humility

Do you think this is an unlikely quality for an entrepreneur? If so, perhaps you have yet to meet a real one. Humility is a word often misunderstood and misused. It has nothing to do with being walked all over; rather it means a genuine desire to be of service to others. It is the hallmark of the true entrepreneur.

Add *munificence* to your personal list of qualities and you will rapidly discover that as you give more by way of added value, your small business will prosper and grow in tandem.

SMOOTHING DOWN THE ROUGH EDGES

The foregoing represent the essential qualities of true entrepreneurship but there are others which you'll find expressed throughout the pages of this book.

Certain of these qualities you may already possess in abundance; others may seem alien to your nature. That's just a first impression and first impressions are not infallible.

For the next week or so concentrate on applying to your everyday dealings those qualities you feel easy with until their application becomes almost second nature. Then spend a full week working on each of the remainder. You won't find the work too difficult. This way you'll gradually smooth down any rough edges that might prevent you being successful in your journey of entrepreneurship.

CASE STUDIES

Tom and Paula progress their strategy

Let's have an update on how Tom and Paula are getting on:

The business plan is now complete and has been circulated to all potential funding sources.

They've had several more meetings with the public sector officials, and while it's slow going, they both feel sure that they're on the right track to securing funding assistance for the enterprise.

Tom's had a few more orders confirmed.

Paula has come to an arrangement with the Skills Funding Agency whereby for a nominal fee (and without long-term commitment) they will rent accommodation facilities: occasional room hire, mail receipt and dispatch, message-taking, fax and secretarial services.

They have both been looking out for suitable permanent premises and have located some likely propositions.

All in all, they are reasonably satisfied with their efforts to date.

Hazel has the collywobbles

The night before the launch of their catering business brought on an unexpected attack of nerves in the normally unflappable Hazel. She was 'feeling the fear' for the first time and collywobbles were starting to get the better of her.

Paul came to the rescue with some words of soothing comfort.

'C'mon kid. This isn't like you, you've been a tower of strength for the past few weeks. We'd never have got this far without your staying power. It's going to be OK. You'll see.'

John and Colin learn not to assume

Day One of the 'Comely Coaches' venture proved eventful. John and Colin were only minutes into their first assignment when the fanbelt snapped. Fortunately, one of the senior citizens on board the coach was a retired mechanic and he volunteered to effect emergency repairs.

The management learned a timely lesson from the episode. As Colin put it, 'Never assume, always check. We'll have to pay more attention to preparation in future.'

ACTION POINTS

1. List the entire range of entrepreneurial qualities you will require to develop in order to be sure of success in your new venture.

2. Name the single greatest quality you can develop.

3. Now make out a list of your own personal qualities, then place them in the order of importance to you. Don't be coy about doing this. You've got good qualities in abundance but maybe you've never given yourself credit for them. Now compare your list with that of the entrepreneur, ticking off those that match. Look at what's left and then start working on them at your own pace.

9
MAINTAINING PROGRESS

To ensure steady progress as you go about your business you must be confident in your ability to control the cash, to negotiate effectively with everyone you come in contact with, to devise strategies for success.

CONTROLLING THE CASH FLOW

Why cash is king

From the moment you start out on a business of your own you must develop the habit of controlling the cash; what you take in, what you pay out. It's called cash flow management.

Don't confuse cash flow with profit. Cash and profit are not the same. Profit includes a number of non-cash items such as depreciation and accruals (costs that you've included but not yet been invoiced for).

Cash flow on the other hand is a simpler concept. It's the balance between the cash you've received (from customers or other sources) less the cash you've paid out (to suppliers and employees). Businesses that go bust do so because they run out of cash, not because they are unprofitable. History records thousands of companies who made paper profits but went bust because they didn't control their cash.

Keeping a cash book

Unlike profit, you can calculate your cash flow at any point in time and do it very quickly. In fact, for the new business venture it is important that you know exactly every day how much cash your business has. This can easily be done by all non-accountants. You simply keep a **cash book** in which you religiously record each day the cash you have received (whether in cash and/or by cheque) and cash that you've paid out (whether in cash and/or by cheque).

There are a number of simple cash book formats available from stationery suppliers, most good high street bookstores and stationery retailers. Alternatively, your accountant will draw up a format that best suits your type of business.

Understanding your cash flow

To many people cash flow has to do with persuading a friendly bank manager to grant an overdraft facility which they've been conditioned to believe will rise and rise and that's the only way you stay in business. This is nonsense.

Getting the cash flow right from the start is critical and keeping it on the right track is even more crucial. But how can you do that if you're not yet self-financing? There is a way, a very sensible way.

☐ You must structure your business in such a way that the bulk of the cash comes in before you have to pay out. That way you'll be working on other people's money, interest free.

I've got such a business. For every project we undertake, we collect 70 per cent of the targeted revenue before we press the button to produce the product. There are many such businesses. Look around and you'll find one.

Keeping your books up to date

Ensuring that your books are always up to date should be a hands-on responsibility for either you or your partner, depending upon which of you possesses the required skills. You may well hire someone to physically 'write up' the books manually or electronically, but one of you should fully understand the process and be directing it. This way you'll always know how your cash flow is performing. Too many start-ups haven't a clue as to how they're doing and usually find out too late to remedy a bad cash flow trend. Don't let that happen to your enterprise.

The books you need

Once again the 'books' you require are simple. All businesses need a **cash book** and a **debtors ledger**. If you have a number of suppliers it's then important that you also record the relevant entries in a **purchase ledger** so that you can easily keep track of what you owe your supply sources and when payment is due. Depending on your type of business – *eg* manufacturing or contract work (plumber, electrician, builder, etc) you may require a **job costing ledger**. The format and completion of this ledger is too involved to discuss here but do ensure that your accountant gives you a thorough briefing on the pros and cons of maintaining these essential records.

Remember, your books are your main source of information. They'll tell you…

☐ how you are doing
☐ what cash you have
☐ what cash you need.

They are also required for inspection by a number of statutory agencies: namely the VAT man and the Inland Revenue, so always keep your books up to date. It's to your advantage in the long run.

Getting some ink on the books

Getting some ink on the books means getting some business in on a regular basis and the only way you'll achieve that is to be out looking every day. A neat set of accounting records may impress your auditor but it won't buy the groceries unless the books are covered in ink – black ink, recording sales transactions and money owed/received.

Hiring an accountant to audit your books

This must be one of your early assignments if you plan to trade as a limited company but look around carefully before deciding. I would recommend you stay away from the bigger practices and opt rather for someone who'll understand your teething problems. You need:

☐ Someone you can trust and get on well with.
☐ Someone who is established in your local area.
☐ Someone who is recommended to you by your bank manager or by a professional colleague.
☐ Someone who is adequately qualified to look after your interests.

Paying your way

By all means take credit (as much as suppliers will allow) but always pay your suppliers on the date you agreed between you at your first meeting. Do this and when the time comes when you need a little more time to pay, you're more likely to have your request granted. It's called trust.

Getting the cash in

I talked about this in some detail in an earlier chapter. If you've forgotten what I said, go back and read it again. Cash coming in less regularly than you're shelling it out spells trouble.

Don't help yourself to the till

In the early days of trading and especially if you are on a roll and the cash is flooding in, it can be very tempting to help yourself occasionally to the till. Avoid this at all costs. It's a mug's game and the only person you'll be robbing is yourself. Till dipping is the most dangerous habit the emerging entrepreneur can fall into because sooner or later you'll have to account for your light fingers and the people you'll have to account to are your creditors.

Trying to trade out of trouble

Trading out of trouble means taking on ever bigger amounts of new business in order to pay off old debts. This is a well-known road to ruin, because your total outstanding debts will simply get bigger and bigger. Avoid the temptation to 'trade your way out of trouble'. Concentrate instead on solving the underlying problems of the business.

 KashFlow is an incredibly easy to understand accounting system for UK small businesses. No accounting knowledge required and the free trial really is free – no credit card needed *http://www.kashflow.co.uk*.

Win-win negotiation tips

Learning how to negotiate removes pressure, stress and friction from your life. Negotiating is like chess – if you don't know how to play you will be intimidated by the activity, especially if your opponent knows the game. Negotiating is a predicable event that has rules, planned moves, and counter moves. But, unlike chess, negotiating is an activity you can't avoid, so learn the rules. This section discusses the five underlying facts about negotiating, win-win negotiating, and the definition of a good negotiator.

Five underlying facts about negotiating

1. **You are negotiating all the time**. Whether you are buying supplies, selling products or services, discussing pay with employees, buying a car, disagreeing with your spouse, or dealing with your children, you are always negotiating. It's just that some of what you negotiate is considered by you as normal activity.

2. **Everything you want is presently owned or controlled by someone else**. Doesn't that statement seem like 'a given?'. But think of the implications. To get what you want means you have to negotiate with the person who has it.

3. **There are predictable responses to strategic manoeuvres or gambits**. It is critical to understand this because if strategies are predictable then they can be managed. If a gambit such as 'nibbling' for extras at the end of a negotiation is employed on you then you can request 'trade-offs' to either stop it or get extras for yourself.

4. **There are three critical factors to every negotiation**:
   The understanding of power – Who has the power in the negotiation? Understanding this will help you in your strategies. Does the person you are dealing with have the power to make the decision? Are you in a weak negotiating position? If so, can you bring in factors or strategies that mitigate that?
   The information factor – What the opponent wants, what they require, and understanding the elements about the object negotiated for are all informational items that are critical for a smooth negotiation or to use to your advantage.
   The time element – Time is an important element to negotiation. If someone wants your product but is desperate because they need it quickly, it's a big factor in the strength of your position. You know they have little time to compare other products. You can guarantee speed for more money.

5. **People are different and have different personality styles that must be accounted for in negotiations**. Strategies are affected by the people within the negotiation. If you play to the needs and desires of the person, you will be more successful in the negotiation.

Win-win negotiating

Understanding the underlying facts about negotiations gives you a base to work from in any negotiation, but win-win is a central theme that must be concentrated on. Keep in mind three simple rules:

1. **Never narrow negotiations down to one issue**. Doing so leaves the participants in the position of having a winner or a loser. When single-issue negotiations become a factor, broaden the scope of the negotiations. If immediate delivery is important to a customer and you can't meet the schedule, maybe a partial shipment will resolve their problem while you produce the rest.

2. **Never assume you know what the other party wants**. What you think you are negotiating for may be totally different from what they are. You may be selling them on quality, when what they need is medium quality, low price and large volume. Always keep an eye on their wants and needs.

3. **Understand that people are different and have different perspectives on negotiations**. Some may want to negotiate and build a long-term business relationship. Others may want the deal, and a handshake and it's over. Price is generally an important factor but never assume that money is the only issue. Other issues can change the price they are willing to accept or the price you are willing to accept, like financing, quality, and speed.

The negotiator

Let's now direct our attention to the negotiator. You. To be a good negotiator requires five things:

1. **Understand that negotiating is always a two-way affair**. If you ignore that fact, you will ignore the needs of the other party and put a stake in the heart of the negotiation.

2. **Desire to acquire the skills of negotiating**. Negotiating is a learned activity. Constantly evaluate your performance and determine how you can improve.

3. **Understand how the human factor and gambits affect negotiating**. Knowing one gambit and using it always is not enough. It may not work on some people. They may have an effective counter to the gambit. Then you are lost or may not recognise tactics being used on you.

4. **Be willing to practise**. Pay attention to what you are doing during negotiations. Plan them and re-evaluate your performance. Prepare for negotiations by practising with someone.

5. **Desire to create win-win situations.** You don't want to negotiate with someone who only wants to destroy you. If you both win, a future deal is possible.

As you understand the rules and the process of negotiations, the stress, pressure and friction that currently get in your way will disappear. You will learn to enjoy the process.

NEGOTIATING SUCCESSFULLY

Every time you negotiate in your business dealings, try to focus on achieving a win-win result – every time. Win-win is good – good for everyone, particularly in a situation of negotiation for survival. Always leave the other person a door to walk in and out of – and some breathing space for yourself to reflect, gird your loins and get back into the action.

Too many business negotiations fall down because neither party is prepared to give way a little, usually from a sense of insecurity. Both sides are afraid of the outcome of giving away even as much as a penny. But what's there to be afraid of? There's always something you can give without suffering too much pain: even a gesture of showing willing or softening up your attitude can prove sufficient to resolve a dispute in a friendly way.

You'll have to develop this negotiating talent – not to be top of the heap but simply to survive in your chosen enterprise.

Alarm Bell

Imagine you are faced with this piece of cutting edge negotiation: you are in receipt of a writ for non-payment of a bill which you are unable to pay right now. Devise a strategy for mollifying the pursuer.

Negotiating to buy

When you're starting out it's no great problem negotiating the right terms for the furniture, computer equipment, pens, pencils, paper and so on that you're going to need to get you going. These suppliers are all engaged in highly competitive markets; they're just as hungry as you are even though they may have been operating successfully for many years.

However, no matter the nature of your particular venture, you'll need to find and then negotiate with regular suppliers who will be essential to the successful functioning of the business. It makes no difference whether you're manufacturing or supplying a service – locating and negotiating successfully with these essential supply sources is vital.

To begin with you'll have to depend heavily on your best asset, *ie* your integrity, coupled with a measure of personal charm. Even if you have a track record in your chosen trade or profession, you'll still have a job to convince regular suppliers that you're going to prove a good credit risk for future dealings.

Remember – particularly at the outset – that negotiation is a two way process. Give a little, take a little... and if you keep on doing that you'll be the one that gets more in every negotiation.

Negotiating to sell

We examined this concept earlier in Chapter 7. Before you read further, flick back for a quick recap on the basic ideas discussed here.

Making it happen

Many negotiations in the exhilarating arena of selling face-to-face falter because the person trying to clinch the sale fails to recognise that things don't just happen; you have to make them happen. Remember the essential work you have to do before you reach the face-to-face interview to get your order approved: researching, prospecting and appointment making. If you sit around too long waiting for inspiration, you'll find the main event slipping away from you to be quickly replaced by gloomy despair. Don't let this happen to you.

Example

This section of the book came together following a visit I made to the south east of England on the negotiation of future publishing contracts. I also managed the time to fit in several 'catch you up' meetings with field sales personnel. One of these in particular inspired this section.

He'd been with the company for only a matter of weeks but his performance to date was quite outstanding. I told him so as soon as we met up but to my surprise he was full of moans and groans together with foreboding about the future. He'd had three good weeks beforehand but (even though it was only Wednesday) was now rapidly convincing himself that he was doomed to drawing a blank this week and worse still, that this was to be the pattern for all nine remaining weeks of the project he was currently working on.

My unhappy operative couldn't wait to let me know how bad things were: he had been assigned to a bad project; it didn't match the profile of the area; the area was much too vast for one man to get results; the results he'd obtained so far were all we could hope to achieve; achievement on the scale I was looking for was quite impossible; 'Impossible', his wife had told him the first day he started ... and so on and so forth.

I listened to him whingeing for 15 minutes until I could stand it no more.

'So, what are you saying? You want out?'

'I didn't say that,' he replied. 'I'm not a quitter. I'll see the project through.'

'What's there to see through? You've convinced yourself that there's nothing left to go for.'

Claiming vehemently that he was not a quitter and wanted to be allowed to continue, he then proceeded to disprove *my* point about *his* assessment of the project, *ie* there would appear to be nothing left to go for (although he couldn't see for himself at the time that he'd actually done rather well and that there was still substantial room for manoeuvre). He'd certainly done his homework on *perceived* self-destruction as he showed by producing reams of statistics in a further effort to convince me of the non-viability of what he was doing, culminating in a performance appraisal which looked like this:

Companies contacted to arrange an appointment	172
'No's' by telephone	50
Outstanding call backs	36
Appointments booked	86 (176)

Appointments completed 73
Sales confirmed.. 31

'No's' face-to-face or subsequently confirmed.. 20

Still considering... 22 (73)

All in all his performance was acceptable measured against the benchmarks of this particular business. His problem was immediately apparent. 'No's' equalled failure and 'considering' represented future failure. He couldn't see the wood for the trees ahead and had decided that the end was nigh.

'You reckon that's it then, do you?', I said. 'Losers 7, winners 1. End of the game, take down the goal posts and go home.'

'No, no... I was hoping that with your experience you'd find me a way back into the action.'

I looked at him in disbelief.

'Who do you take me for, son? Svengali, Houdini, one of those guys? You present me with what you regard as a scenario for disaster and you want me to show you the way out. How long have I got?...'

What we did then was to sit down and evaluate his moans and groans to establish which of them we could do something about and which weren't even worthy of discussion, ending up with an evaluation of his own performance appraisal.

What came out of the latter exercise was positive proof that he'd done rather well despite his misgivings and that there was plenty of room for improvement. The conversion factor of 42.47 per cent on confirmed sales to face-to-face appointments was excellent and I was able to persuade him that 'considering' didn't necessarily mean 'no' but rather perhaps 'maybe', 'not now', 'later'. We put this to the test that very afternoon. We called on six of these pending transactions and walked away with a further four sales to make his efforts for the week look more respectable.

'That was brilliant,' said my now re-invigorated operative as we left the last appointment. 'I wish I had your magic.'

'There is no magic. It's all down to application and negotiation. You'd have got those four sales by yourself if you'd been negotiating effectively.'

That's the truth of the matter as we found in the conversation that followed. After a few rebuffs earlier in the week he had fallen into the trap of convincing himself that 'no' and 'considering' equalled failure. He'd also lost sight of several options at his disposal for immediately turning round these initial reactions into confirmed sales: second advertisement colour thrown in free of charge, discounts and (but only as a last resort) deferred payment. The sales we obtained that afternoon were all clinched on painless negotiation: free second colour to seal an early deal.

Be prepared to negotiate every deal with the tools at your disposal when you are up against initial resistance.

Negotiating your selling policies

It's your privilege to create the policies that set your selling prices but always try to be flexible by negotiating with everyone connected with the process: with yourself on occasion. That's fine as long as the end result is the protection (or improvement) of your margins.

Marketing effectively through negotiation

When you've read this book in its entirety go back again and study Chapter 6, 'Marketing Your Enterprise'. Observe how the negotiation process runs through every strand of activity contained therein in the effective marketing of your business. No one expects you to be a marketing guru when you first start out but some wide boys you will meet along the way may try to take advantage of the learning curve you'll be on for some time.

Never take anything at face value. Always try to work out the true value of what's on offer through common sense and by consistently negotiating with admen, designers, printers and the like.

Negotiating with your bank manager

I recently attended a useful hour long seminar sponsored by the bank my company uses. It was aptly entitled 'How to Handle Your Bank Manager'. Basically it was all about effective negotiation *before* the problems arise. Negotiating with the bank manager *before* you need additional funding, *before* presenting downturned year-end accounts, *before* the need to extend the overdraft.

Negotiating for your cash flow

Always remember the absolute necessity of continuous negotiation with both your debtors and creditors in order to ensure a viable cash flow for your business. Unless you negotiate, your cash flow will always be at the mercy of both your customers and your suppliers. That sort of diminished control spells disaster in the long run.

Negotiation through networking

Another useful way of extending your negotiation skills is through commercial networking; for example through:

- ☐ Rotary Clubs
- ☐ Chambers of Commerce
- ☐ Business Clubs
- ☐ Trade Associations.

These entities are always on the lookout for additional recruits and if you are gregariou
prepared to serve on committees) joining one that best suits your own field can yield
dividends.

If you can get up on your feet and talk at a moment's notice on a variety of topics, you could
also join the local speaker forum.

You could even write a book...

SUCCEEDING THROUGH STRATEGY

You'll not only ensure success for your new venture but you'll enjoy that success sooner than
otherwise if you develop the practice of creating individual strategies for all your endeavours.
Strategies for everything.

Making good use of your business plan

Your business plan is your very first attempt at strategic planning. It explains:

- □ what your idea is all about
- □ how it works in practice
- □ how you will set about raising the required funding
- □ what you'll do with the funding when you get it
- □ what profit levels you are aiming to achieve
- □ how you'll market your venture

and a whole manner of other essentials for successful trading.

Don't leave your business plan lying about gathering dust once you're up and running. Feed
it into your word processor and discipline yourself to its regular updating. This plan is your
core tool for strategic planning. Change and develop its contents in tandem with the
progress of your enterprise. Don't leave it until the end of the year, or even quarterly. Update
it at each month-end and if you can't find the time to do it yourself, delegate this vital task to
your partner. It's no use popping in to ask the bank manager for additional funding three
years hence with a three year old plan, even if you're doing exceptionally well. He'll just send
you away until you get it up to speed.

Developing a strategy for everything

Over the years I've developed the habit of never undertaking *anything* in my personal or
business life without first committing to paper a strategy for its successful conclusion.
Properly constructed strategies are essential for efficiency: they establish what your purpose
is in any undertaking, what you are planning to ultimately achieve and what you might be
prepared to agree to in a tricky negotiation. Strategies also help you get there faster.

Strategies for everything? Surely that involves a great deal of time and effort? Not at all. Once
you get the hang of it you can develop strategies on the back of an envelope, the blank space

in the 'Stop Press' column of your evening newspaper or even (as I've done on many occasions) the reverse side of till receipts.

Strategies for tricky situations

When you're faced with a difficult piece of negotiation always turn up with your own carefully constructed strategy for resolving it effectively. You may think you've already got the answer in your head but if you fail to commit it to paper beforehand (just one A4 sheet will suffice) you may be in for a pasting. Chances are the other party has a written strategy secreted somewhere easily accessible in that bulging file.

What do you include in this single sheet of A4 to construct an effective strategy? – Just the salient points will do. But set it out in such a way as to provide for easy reference, cross reference, balance and counterbalance as discussion ensues. You let your guard down every time you resort to raking through files to find a trump card.

Example

Let's take a hypothetical example and draw up a strategy to manage the situation:

You're about to place an order for £100,000 worth of essential equipment but you have an uneasy feeling about both the deal and the suppliers. You can't point to anything in particular as to why you should feel this way, but as you think about it there are one or two aspects that need clarification before you sign on the dotted line.

Here's what you do with your A4 sheet.

REDCAR ENGINEERING EQUIPMENT PURCHASE

Positive Factors	*Negative Factors*
1. Price seems fair (but could we negotiate for better terms or deferred payment?)	1. Service package too loosely defined. Needs clarification.
2. Sound company with 30 years' experience in the industry.	2. Don't feel comfortable with Production Director. Ask about his background. Find out how long he's been with the company.
3. Guaranteed delivery dates.	3. How strong is the guarantee? Ask for belt and braces security.
4. Only company around who can handle a job this big.	4. Is this *really* true?

Conclusion
1. We haven't done our homework thoroughly.
2. We had better get total clarification before proceeding.

Action
1. Hammer them for improved price and terms.
2. Don't commit until negative factors are eliminated.

Option
Leave the entire deal on ice for another month, while we source elsewhere.

Laying out the pluses and minuses in this fashion coupled with conclusions, potential action and options allows you to focus on the main menu while flicking back and forth for balance and counterbalance in your discussion.

Strategies for controlling meetings

Never ever engage in any meeting with anyone without first preparing a strategy for control. If you don't do this you are in danger of being both rolled over and railroaded.

When anyone mentions the word 'meeting' to me I switch on automatically to a little list indelibly impressed on my conscious mind (although I do have a written version in my pocket in the event of a power failure). It goes like this:

- ☐ Who's calling this meeting?
- ☐ Why?
- ☐ What's the *real* purpose behind it?
- ☐ What's on the agenda?
- ☐ Is there a hidden agenda I don't know about?
- ☐ What's in it for me?
- ☐ What's the best I could hope to achieve?
- ☐ What would I settle for?

Sounds suspicious? – But it pays to get as many facts together as you can before participating. This way you're more likely to be the one in control.

How to conduct effective meetings

1. **Have somebody in charge who people respect and will defer to** for better or for worse. This is the most efficient way.

2. **Have key attendees have something to report, not just discuss**. This creates ownership and responsibility.

3. **Do most of the work of the meeting *before* the meeting itself**. It's hard to get work done, alliances made or problems solved during a meeting – take care of most of this 1:1 before the meeting itself.

4. **Start the meeting on time, every time** and, don't accept comments from those who are late. People will learn soon enough to be on time.

5. **Schedule some meetings without formalised agendas**. These would include brainstorming sessions, open forums, etc. A formal agenda would squelch input and creativity. A highly valuable meeting doesn't have to be oriented around or justified by a preset agenda!

6. **Schedule random meetings, not just regular ones**. Staff meetings at 8am every Monday, don't always work well. People get into a routine, get bored, etc. Schedule meetings designed to accomplish something.

7. **Have the first 15 minutes as catch-up time; then get into the meeting**. Warm everyone up by casual chatter for the first part of the meeting. This releases any pent up energy in the room, leaving participants more open.

8. **Schedule telemeetings and chat meetings, not just in-person meetings**. Some meetings work better if they aren't in person or onsite. Use teleconferencing and web chat rooms when possible.

9. **Don't make the meeting a production**. Slides are cool; handouts are nice. But they are expensive and may not really cause the type of input or collaboration that meetings are best for. Ask yourself: 'Am I trying to educate/impress/enroll people or do I need their help to solve/create something?' If the former, do the dog and pony show; if the latter, don't.

10. **Label the type of meeting it's going to be in the announcement memo**. Is the meeting going to be a dialogue or a reporting session, brainstorming opportunity, value-added session, problem-solving one – or a crisis discussion? Give attendees the context for the meeting, not just the time, date, location and agenda.

Strategies for success

Basically, every strategy you evolve as you go about your business affairs should be a strategy for success – otherwise there would be no point in bothering to produce them. In other words, your strategies must:

☐ be positive in their outlook
☐ examine problematic aspects objectively
☐ arrive at conclusions
☐ pose options
☐ suggest initial action.

If you keep at it, you'll soon find that strategy making comes naturally to you in your everyday dealings and that success comes sooner rather than later.

Strategies for survival

Even established concerns which have been successfully trading for many years can sometimes reach a stage when creating a strategy for survival suddenly becomes imperative. This can happen overnight for a variety of unforeseen circumstances: market evaporation, product obsolescence, price wars and the like.

This is unlikely to happen to you in the beginning but as you progress, always be prepared for the possibility.

You can develop strategies for any eventuality but here's one you might want to give consideration to if you haven't yet committed to starting out on your own. Maybe giving up your current career is a worry to you, maybe you just want to taste and see.

Strategies for piloting a new business

Constructing a strategy for launching a new business on a part-time pilot basis is something I wouldn't recommend lightly. However, since I recently completed that task for a friend, I will touch on it here. There is nothing wrong with piloting your venture in advance, as long as you treat the exercise as if it were to be your bread and butter without any jam on top.

Here are a few factors to bear in mind before committing yourself to a pilot operation:

☐ Refine your business plan accordingly.

☐ Don't allow for any external funding except perhaps from your bank manager who might be prepared to lend on a fully secured basis.

☐ Treat the following as if you were going full-time:
  – corporate image
  – market research
  – pricing policy
  – marketing programme
  – sales strategy.

☐ Consider carefully before opting to pilot from home on a part-time basis. The bank won't much like it and neither will your suppliers and customers. Your best route is to get a temporary base at a recognised business centre.

BOOSTING YOUR DECISION-MAKING PROWESS

Just as people are different, so are their styles of decision making. Each person is a result of all of the decisions made in their life to date. Recognising this, here are some tips to enhance your decision-making batting average.

☐ Do not make decisions that are not yours to make.

☐ When making a decision you are simply choosing from among alternatives. You are not making a choice between right and wrong.

- ☐ Avoid snap decisions. Move fast on the reversible ones and slowly on the non-reversible.

- ☐ Choosing the right alternative at the wrong time is not any better than the wrong alternative at the right time, so make the decision while you still have time.

- ☐ Do your decision making on paper. Make notes and keep your ideas visible so you can consider all the relevant information in making this decision.

- ☐ Be sure to make a choice based on what is right, not who is right.

- ☐ Write down the pros and cons of a line of action. It clarifies your thinking and makes for a better decision.

- ☐ Make decisions as you go along. Do not let them accumulate. A backlog of many little decisions could be harder to deal with than one big and complex decision.

- ☐ Consider those affected by your decision. Whenever feasible, get them involved to increase their commitment.

- ☐ Recognise that you cannot know with 100 per cent certainty that your decision is correct because the actions to implement it are to take place in the future. So make it and don't worry about it.

- ☐ Use the OAR approach in decision making. Look at O, **O**bjectives you are seeking to attain, A, the **A**lternatives you sense are available to you and R, the **R**isk of the alternative you are considering.

- ☐ It has been said that a decision should always be made at the lowest possible level and as close to the scene of action as possible. However, a decision should always be made at a level ensuring that all activities and objectives affected are fully considered. The first rule tells us how far down a decision should be made. The second how far down it can be made.

- ☐ Remember that not making a decision is a decision not to take action.

- ☐ To be effective, a manager must have the luxury of having the right to be wrong.

- ☐ Trust yourself to make a decision and then to be able to field the consequences appropriately.

- ☐ Don't waste your time making decisions that do not have to be made.

- ☐ Determine alternative courses of action before gathering data.

- ☐ Before implementing what appears to be the best choice, assess the risk by asking 'What can I think of that might go wrong with this alternative?'

- ☐ Many decisions you make are unimportant (about 80 per cent of them). Establish operating limits and let your secretary or others make them for you.

- ☐ Consider making the decision yourself in lieu of a group, but recognise the potential for less commitment by those affected.

- ☐ As part of your decision-making process, always consider how the decision is to be implemented.

- ☐ As soon as you are aware that a decision will have to be made on a specific situation, review the facts at hand then set it aside. Let this incubate in your subconscious mind until it is time to finally make the decision.

- ☐ Once the decision has been made, don't look back. Be aware of how it is currently affecting you and focus on your next move. Never regret a decision. It was the right thing to do at the time. Now focus on what is right at this time.

- ☐ Mentally rehearse the implementation of your choice and reflect in your imagination what outcomes will result.

- ☐ Brainstorming alternative solutions with your staff or others will gain fresh ideas and commitment.

- ☐ Discontinue prolonged deliberation about your decision. Make it and carry it through.

- ☐ Once you have made the decision and have started what you are going to do, put the 'what if's' aside and do it with commitment.

FEELING THE FEAR

As you walk the unfamiliar roads to starting an enterprise for the first time, it's only natural to feel the collywobbles taking hold now and again. But fear is only an emotion and if you understand and handle it correctly it can be useful to you.

That sinking feeling

You found your idea, you wrote a brilliant plan, your plan got you your funding, you launched your enterprise and here you are on your first day sitting at your brand new (second-hand) desk surveying your empire.

What are you feeling right now?

The chances are you'll have a sinking sensation in your gut and feel scared witless. Don't be alarmed. It's all part of the experience of entrepreneurship. The solution is to get off your desk, out of your office, meet lots of people and start selling. There is nothing like a few calls and a few early wins to settle you down. Leave as much paperwork as you can to your partner.

Every time you feel the collywobbles coming back, repeat the exercise.

The positive side of fear

Left to its own devices, even the slightest fear will very quickly turn into worry and worry eventually into panic. Identify your fears as they occur; look them straight in the eye and analyse them. They will relate to one of two things: things you can do something about, things you can do nothing about. Forget the latter and concentrate on that for which you can do something, *anything* to put right.

This is the positive side of fear. Use it always and you'll have nothing to fear. At the height of the depression in the early 1930s President Roosevelt admonished the citizens of the United States with these words of wisdom, 'We have nothing to fear but fear itself.' He was right and went on to prove it, and gradually confidence returned.

Addressing problematic situations

Practise addressing problems as soon as fear arises, and very soon you'll find that you are not only addressing them confidently but solving them fearlessly and successfully.

Clearing the hurdles

There are truthfully very few hurdles you will meet in your journey of entrepreneurship that you cannot overcome somehow or other. In the beginning molehills can look like mountains. Just sit down, analyse the problem, discard the impossible and get on with that which can be done.

AVOIDING COSTLY MISTAKES THAT CRIPPLE SMALL BUSINESS

The power-laden strategies you are absorbing as you course through the pages of this book are all devised from quantifiable mistakes that have pulled down many a promising enterprise. Whether you have been in business for years or are just starting out, you need to recognise these costly errors before you can avoid them. These, then, are the deadly traps that too many small business owners fall into.

1. **Getting wedded to an idea and sticking with it for too long**. Don't stay married for life to a single idea. Ideas are the currency of entrepreneurs. Play around with as many ideas as you like to discover which ones create money and lasting success.

2. **Operating without a viable marketing plan**. A winning marketing plan captures the attention you need to surround your enterprise with the right calibre of people: employees, customers, suppliers. There may be a hundred disparate ways to market your business but an exclusive viable plan implemented effectively, efficiently, and consistently will be results driven, eliminating guesswork.

3. **Failing to appreciate market forces**. Changes in customer preferences and advances in competitive products and services can leave you stranded in the dust unless you take the trouble to get to know your market and your customers well. It is essential that you appreciate what customers want now, what they're likely to want in the future, how

their buying patterns are evolving, and how you can become a constant resource for them even if you don't have the right products and services for them right now.

4. **Ignoring your cash position**. Customers do not always respond to superior products in the time frame that you think they should. You'll need plenty of cash to sustain operations in the interim. Cash is king, so be on your guard as to how it flows in – and out.

5. **Ignoring employees**. The management and motivation of staff is one of the biggest challenges facing the business owner. Without patience, persistence and people skills, problems quickly multiply – and morale, productivity and profits can easily be destroyed. Always make your people your first priority.

6. **Confusing likelihood with reality**. The successful entrepreneur lives in the world of likelihood but spends money in the real world. Be realistic in all of your commercial undertakings.

7. **Operating without a sales strategy**. Without a strategy for selling, there is no effective way to gauge the financial growth and progress of a business. You need a realistic map that identifies where the sales will come from, how they will come – and from whom.

8. **Playing the Lone Ranger with no back up**. You are the key to it all but you cannot do everything yourself and continue to grow at the same time. Even modest success can overwhelm you unless you hire the right staff *and* delegate responsibility.

9. **Operating with no mastermind on board**. Most small businesses expand faster when there is someone around with a few grey hairs to cast an experienced eye occasionally on overall activity. Your elder statesperson could operate for you as an executive director or part-time consultant.

10. **Giving up**. Not every successful entrepreneur gets it right first time; some fail several times before they strike the core formula that does it for them. So, if you are failing, go ahead and fail. But fail fast and learn from the experience. Then try again with this new wisdom. Never give up and never suffer either.

Knowledge is the key

The birds of the air have the knowledge (and the wings) to get from one destination to another on time, every time. They have no need of travel schedules, passports, currency exchange, traveller cheques, or any other restrictive man-made paraphernalia to delay their progress. Flocks of swifts, for example, are so confident of their navigational prowess they catnap on the wing on journeys spanning thousands of miles. They have an instinctive fail-safe route plan.

So, too, will you when you have absorbed the strategies set out in this book because you will have the knowledge and the wings to avoid the ten most deadly mistakes in minding your own business.

THE GOLDEN RULE OF PERSONAL INTEGRITY

Your personal integrity is, and will always remain, the *most vital* asset of the new enterprise you are planning to launch. This personal quality is more vital to you than all the funding you will raise, more vital than 100 confirmed orders to get you going.

Nurture and protect your integrity in all your dealings. What you say you will do, you must do – even if it costs you. If you make a mistake that produces a downside for someone else, put your hands up immediately and admit to it. Then do everything in your power to rectify matters.

Being honest with yourself

Above all, be honest with yourself. It's easy to convince yourself that things are OK when they're patently not. Address all of your problems as soon as they arise and deal with them with courage and integrity.

The secret of success in business is personal integrity. Everything else is down to application. Never forget that.

NEVER ALLOW YOUR ROUTE TO THE TOP TO BE COMPROMISED

Maintaining progress in small business can be severely compromised when you take on too much. Work overload sets in and unless you learn how to handle it your route to the top will be blocked; doubt, anxiety, panic move rapidly into any situation that is getting out of control. This 13-point strategy appeared in the 'Brainfood' section of the August 2004 edition of *Management Today*. Try it – it works.

Stop and think. It's easy to panic and launch yourself at the task in hand without considering the most sensible course of action. A few moments of reflection and planning pay off.

Break the situation down into chunks. Picturing the whole task makes it look terrifying; small steps are manageable.

Delegate. There may be people around you who can help and offer expertise – take it.

Manage expectations. You may need to explain to others that the end result might be different from initial expectations. Better to bite the bullet early on and enlist help than give people a nasty surprise when you pass the point of no return.

Consider urgency and importance. The danger is to rush around doing the urgent things but ignoring the important ones. If something is both urgent and important, act. If not, prioritise.

Start small. Focus on getting some quick results as this will give you momentum.

Develop a contingency plan. Even in the most difficult situations there are options.

Go for the 80/20 rule. Build the stadium without the roof; write the report without the annotated footnotes.

Don't be too hard on yourself. Having decided what to focus on, do not worry about things you're not going to do. Put your energies into finishing everything else to a high standard.

Talk to your team. If everybody knows what is happening, less time will be spent on unproductive action. Consider creating a war room where people know action is being taken.

Communicate to interested parties. It's better to lead the communication of a crisis than being forced to respond to someone else's interpretations.

Remember it will pass. Life is bigger than a wobbly project.

Learn from the situation for next time. Patterns can turn into habits. If you're aware of what led to the situation, you can catch it before it happens again.

CASE STUDIES

Paula cautions Tom

Tom and Paula are on the home stretch now. The public sector funding is in position and they've even found a friendly banker who on the strength of their efforts to date is prepared to grant them an overdraft of £5,000 against an insurance policy on Tom's life.

The business has lift off, it's trading and the best is yet to come. Six weeks into the first phase of trading, Tom and Paula stepped back and reviewed their activities to date.

All in all, there was a lot to be pleased about: the order book was filling up, the first few completed projects had received critical acclaim from the clients and there had been no serious mechanical breakdowns.

However, Paula cautioned Tom that job costings would have to be looked at more carefully from now on as overall profitability was being impaired by some slack estimating.

Paul's wagon rolls

'All work and no play makes Paul a plonker. Let's take some time off, Hazel, and spend a few days away from the van. We can afford it now.'

And afford it they could as Hazel subsequently confirmed.

They talked to Hazel's dad that evening and he readily agreed to fill in for them while they were away.

The business had taken off, it was already into profit and the young entrepreneurs were learning that rest is as important as activity when you're running your own show.

Business booms for Colin and John

John and Colin had just left the offices of the Skills Funding Agency following a review meeting on their progress. They were relaxing over a pint in the 'Feathers'.

'The business development people seem quite happy with the way things are panning out,' said Colin.

'Yes,' replied John. 'Else they wouldn't be talking about introducing us to some possible new contracts. If we carry on at this rate we'll both be back on PAYE before too long...'

ACTION POINTS

1. Pinpoint exactly when the collywobbles are first likely to strike you in your enterprise.

2. Highlight the positive use you can make of feelings of fear.

3. Describe how you will tackle problematic situations.

4. Place a value on your personal integrity in business.

5. Write down all the things you reckon might cause you most anxiety about setting up in business for yourself. Carefully examine each of them in detail. If you spend some time on this exercise, and do it calmly, you will find yourself providing most of the answers before discussing the matter with anyone else. Those that defy an acceptable solution, leave aside for a while, then try another way around or ask a fellow professional for advice.

10
POWERING YOUR WAY TO SUCCESS

There are several things you can do to accelerate your progress and power your way to success. The tools you will need won't cost a penny: you already possess them. They are all within you and just waiting to be asked. These tools are priceless and they are yours to use whenever you please. Access is easy because they are all in your mind.

YOUR SECRET POWERS

Maximising your mindpower

Human mindpower is awesome. We all live in a mind world; how each of us sees in our mind's eye just what's happening out there in the real world actually makes it how it is. We look at the world through our eyes and immediately make judgements solely on the evidence of our eyes. In other words we start interpreting situations as soon as they occur in our lives. If we're not careful, mindpower can work against us if we fall into the bad habit of always looking for negative aspects in our daily experiences.

Try always to use mindpower effectively by the continuous application of positive thought and action. Events rarely 'are' as they seem, so wouldn't it pay you to look for the good in every situation?

Napoleon Hill, the American entrepreneur and author, is credited with the famous saying, 'What the mind can conceive and believe, the mind can achieve.'

Maximising your brain power

Your brain is equally awesome, more awesome than the most powerful computer ever invented or still to be conceived. It can translate into action all your ideas, and achieve your every scenario, ambition, and daydream.

Those who know about such things reckon that on average we use only one tenth of this power in finding our way around life. How much more efficient we would all become by increasing this percentage by just another five points.

Try maximising on your brainpower in every aspect of your new venture.

Drawing on the power within

Your mind operates on three distinct levels:

- [ ] conscious
- [ ] subconscious
- [ ] superconscious (or supraconscious).

We all know about the first two but what do we know about the third level? Very little by all accounts. What is known, though, is that those who develop the power of drawing occasionally on this level of consciousness open the floodgates to inspiration and prosperity.

Many people can testify to having occasionally touched upon the wisdom of the superconscious and so brought a little magic into their lives.

There are some excellent books available on the subject of mind power. Investigate for yourself, and start drawing on this power within yourself.

Drawing on spiritual energy

Call it what you will but there is an energy available to you, an energy generating through God, the Universal Force, the Power or whatever else you might wish to call it. Drawing upon this spiritual energy is easy although it does require continuous application on your part.

You owe it to yourself and to those around you to make the best of yourself, your mind and your brain. Life has a wonderful way of rewarding those who use their best endeavours in all they undertake.

Using your mindpower to overcome

No matter what your age or personal circumstances you can effectively use the magic of mindpower to achieve whatever targets you set yourself.

I had to rely almost entirely on mindpower when planning the launch of my company. I had no money, no resources, no income; and it looked as if my future was already behind me. I would have been sunk, unless I had developed a mind-set fixed firmly to achieving the targets I'd set myself.

Alarm Bell

You have just read how at the start of my enterprise I conquered lack of finance, resources, and income. What is the worst that could happen to you and how would you triumph over perceived shortcomings?

Is age the problem?

Far too many people get hung up on the vexing question of age. How old (or how young) do you feel? That's how old or young you are, no more, no less. Of course you will meet prejudices along the way but what of it? Your age in numerical terms (and that's really all people are bothered about) is nobody's business but yours. Saw a few years off, if that makes you feel more relaxed, but never ever add any on, even if you think you're too young. Confusing, isn't it?

Use mindpower to set your *real* age in terms of maturity and then get cracking by using mindpower and precious time in tandem to achieve your dreams.

Is money the problem?

'Well, of course it is!' I can hear you saying. Isn't it always? But remember, your mind can work miracles. So, if shortage of cash to get you going is the problem, put your mind to work on finding a solution. There's no shortage of money in this world, just a void of information on locating it when you really need it. Let go, and let your mind lead you to it.

Is rejection the problem?

Don't allow constant rejection to get you down. It's a waste of time and energy. Fix your mind on what *you* want, and not on what *they* won't allow you to have. Remember, we live in a mind world. Make sure the environment in your mind is healthily compatible with your ambition and desires.

Is redundancy the problem?

If redundancy is the problem, then do as Tom did. Do something about it. Use mindpower to get you where you want to be. If no one else has the foresight to hire you, put your skills and that great mind to work to set yourself up in a profitable business of your own.

Is frustration the problem?

Did you retire too early? Are you in a secure salaried position but bursting to get out on your own? Frustration can eat away at you like a cancer. Don't allow it to happen to you. Get your mind on the case.

MOVING MOUNTAINS

As you are going through the initial machinations of convincing people about your business plan, attracting the interest of public sector funding sources and the banks, finding a suitable partner and locating premises, you may have to nudge the occasional molehill to get what you want.

When you are up and running and have been trading successfully for some time you will sometimes find yourself facing several mountains that require moving at once, or several doors to push open.

The three sisters of success

The tools you will need for these monumental tasks are the three 'Sisters of Success': faith, hope and love.

By faith, I mean boundless belief in human potential – not only your own potential but that of all the people you will meet and deal with in your business life.

Whatever else you may risk losing on your journey of entrepreneurship, you must never lose hope. Hope will see you through all the toughest and worse situations. Some of the most powerful stories in human life concern the triumph of hope over adversity.

And love? – What has 'love' to do with business? Love means placing the highest value on everything and everyone. You'll need lots of this if you're going to build a business that you and everyone around you will be proud of: love of hard work, love for your employees, love for your customers, love for your suppliers, even love for your competitors, and a love of the person you wish to become.

> Razor-sharp *Intuition* is a wonderful tool to have at your disposal when faced with vexatious problems. Email *jimgreen@writing-for-profit.com* with INTUITION in the subject line and I'll send you a useful mp3 tool.

ARE YOU READY?

We are more than half way through this book which I hope is providing an insight into what it takes to start your own enterprise, regardless of age, circumstances, money, retirement, rejection or any other obstacle. Here now is a candid quiz to help you discover whether you've got what it really takes.

A self-assessment questionnaire

1. Does the sun only shine for you when things are going well? ☐

2. Can you handle adversity as well as success? ☐

3. Will borrowing to invest in yourself put you off your sleep at night? ☐

4. When people say 'no' can you go back again and ask for a 'yes'? ☐

5. Would you sacrifice your social activities in the quest for excellence? ☐

6. Do you find something (anything) good in everyone you meet? ☐

7. Are you easily offended? ☐

8. Will you freely share your expertise with those you employ? ☐

9. Do you always admit to your mistakes? ☐

10. Could you start again if it all went down the pan? ☐

To score
Score 3 points if you answered 'no' to questions 1, 3 and 7 and 0 points if you answered 'yes'. Score 3 points each time you answered 'yes' to all the others and 0 points if you answered 'no'.

Assessment

0–24:   You are not really ready for the challenge.

24–27: Work on yourself – you can make it.

30:     You can and will make it.

Total mastery of the ten elements that comprise the questionnaire is vital to:

- ☐ launching a successful enterprise
- ☐ developing it from strength to strength
- ☐ getting rich
- ☐ getting lots of fun out of it in the process.

Analysing your score

Does the sun only shine for you when things are going well?
If so, then in the words of a very old song, you've got to develop the habit of looking for the silver lining in every cloud. Things are rarely as bad as they seem. It's a case of (in the words of another old song) accentuating the positive and eliminating the negative. Positive thinkers are winners. Negative thinkers are losers.

Can you handle adversity as well as success?
Being in business for yourself is a whole way of life. It is full of peaks and troughs, successes and failures. The winners handle every outcome, good or bad, with the same equanimity. Winning is great, losing is awful, but neither experience is the final word. When you fail to make a sale or tie up a contract, ask yourself why. You'll learn something to your advantage which will make you much better able to succeed next time.

Will borrowing to invest in yourself put you off your sleep at night?
You may be lucky enough not to have to borrow to start off, but somewhere along the way you may have to borrow in order to expand. Does the prospect of that worry you? Think hard about it before you take the plunge.

When people say 'no' can you go back again and ask for a 'yes'?
When people say 'no', they very often mean 'not now' or 'later maybe'. In other words, they weren't ready for whatever reason when you asked them. Always be prepared to go back and ask again for a 'yes'. The worst than can happen is you get another 'no'. Then go back yet again and ask for a 'yes'.

How far would you sacrifice your social activities in the quest for excellence?
You might be surprised how many people wouldn't sacrifice any. If you go about things the right way you'll have so much fun doing business with people that you won't have a lot of time left for pure 'socialising'.

Do you find something good in everyone you meet?
Even the worst of us have merits in our make-up. Practise finding something of value in

everyone you meet. It has much to do with the ability to communicate with people at every level. If you do not feel very good at this, work on it. You will need this ability to succeed.

Are you easily offended?
There is nothing intrinsically wrong if you are, but you're going to meet one or two nasties along the way and you've got to learn how to deal with them. Look for the 'good', and if that doesn't work, rise above events. Whatever, never lose your cool.

Will you freely share your expertise with those you employ?
Lots of employers won't, as a matter of misguided principle. But if you're going to develop fully, you're going to have to share your expertise. You'll run the risk of having someone trying to steal your intellectual property (it rarely comes to anything) but it's a risk well worth taking.

Do you always admit to your mistakes?
You'll be found out pretty quickly if you don't. Be really honest and open in all your dealings with customers, staff and suppliers alike. Personal integrity is your prime asset. You must always protect it.

Could you start all over again if it all went down the pan?
I did, and I can tell you this; I came out of it a stronger and better person. If (God forbid) it happened again, I would certainly make another comeback. Could you?

Success, after all, is only failure turned inside out.

ACTUAL CASE STUDY

Here now is an *actual* case study to help you assess for yourself how all the pieces discussed in the previous chapters actually fit together in a real start-up scenario. The only such case study I'm familiar with is my own, so let's have a look at what occurred in my situation over a 13-month period in the build-up to the business taking off.

Month 1: at the starting point
- plan of action determined on the day of redundancy
- visits to Natwest and Barclays to obtain their Start-Up Packs
- the first strands of the business plan begin to take shape
- work begins on company aims, name and logo.

This was a very difficult time for me: personal tragedy coupled with a severe lack of basic funding didn't make for an ideal start to my adventure. However, the steely qualities in Chapter 8 (in particular persistence and obduracy) saw me safely through the starting gate.

Month 2: progressing the plan
- progression of business plan
- initial outlines for profit & loss and cashflow

- ☐ search begins for information technology tuition
- ☐ start sourcing refresher course on entrepreneurship.

Applying myself to the development of the business plan was both therapeutic and a labour of love but I struggled over the financial projections and had to resort to some wild blue yondering. Sourcing the tuition I badly needed was a bind at the time but persuasion paid off in the end. Other essential qualities employed: ambition and endurance.

Month 3: putting the wheels in motion

- ☐ find, enrol on and start 13-week information technology course
- ☐ accepted for entrepreneurship programme
- ☐ initial appointments with small business advisers (Natwest/Barclays)
- ☐ initial contact with public sector funding sources
- ☐ first draft of business plan completed.

The activities listed above were enacted with speed of application and successfully accomplished with the help of several other essential qualities: persistence, persuasion and decisiveness.

Month 4: tapping on the doors of the funders

- ☐ approaches to more banks for commercial funding
- ☐ technology training, all day Monday to Friday
- ☐ entrepreneurship programme, two evenings weekly
- ☐ second draft of business plan completed.

Month 4 was a period of hard slog when I knew for sure that nothing tangible was about to happen for quite some time. The keynote quality required was patience.

Month 5: identifying an equity partner

- ☐ identify future equity partner
- ☐ revamp elements of business plan
- ☐ partner produces realistic financial projections
- ☐ identify essential suppliers
- ☐ first major public sector funding meeting
- ☐ search begins for premises.

The hard slog continued but I could see several pieces of the jigsaw beginning to shape up which enabled me to move up a gear, emboldened me to progress the masterplan more quickly than I had imagined some months before. Qualities that helped: persistence, decisiveness and confidence.

Month 6: looking for premises

- ☐ complete the technology course
- ☐ premises search continues
- ☐ second public sector funding meeting

☐ start calling on potential customer base
☐ company incorporated.

No gargantuan strides forward quite yet but enthusiasm for the project was beginning to take over and the brick walls ahead didn't look too tough because the adrenaline was starting to flow.

Month 7: seed capital

☐ £10,000 seed capital secured (loans against insurance policies)
☐ minor breakthrough on funding – £3,000 DTI grant approved
☐ final version of business plan completed
☐ public sector funding meetings intensify
☐ presentation to LEC (Local Enterprise Council)
☐ entrepreneurship programme ends.

Still a long way to go but I felt I'd grasped the nettle and it wasn't stinging too badly. My confidence was growing daily and I was becoming more and more articulate in presenting the case for my project.

Month 8: knockback from the banks

☐ temporary accommodation arranged with government agency
☐ knockbacks from all banks approached
☐ intensify customer calls activity.

Locating an accommodation facility was a bonus and the initial thumbs down from the banks neither came as a surprise nor worried me. I was beginning to enjoy being back out there in the field again sowing the seeds for future action with my old customers. Playing its part during Month 8 was persuasion coloured with a touch of style.

Month 9: first piece of business

☐ start trading
☐ invitations to tender on several projects
☐ first contract won
☐ further meetings with public sector funders.

Things were looking good now: up and running, tangible interest from the prospective clientele, a definite order and some sniffing around on the funding front. My confidence was starting to soar.

Month 10: swings and roundabouts

☐ invitations to tender on two major assignments
☐ customer calls intensify
☐ more public sector meetings (seem to be going backwards)
☐ knockbacks from all Month 9 tenders
☐ start discussions on strategic alliance with print house in the event of failure to attract sufficient funding.

Month 10 began brilliantly . . . and then wouldn't you just know . . . There was a major project ready to start immediately but where was the funding to see it through to fruition? A little panic set in causing a decision to instigate preliminary discussions on a strategic alliance with an established print house. Thankfully nothing came of this. The quality that saw us through: obduracy.

Month 11: time to worry

- ☐ ominous silence from all funding sources
- ☐ reject offer on strategic alliance
- ☐ extend catchment area on customer calls.

Time to worry indeed. We'd done everything right, we had an order of sufficient worth to prove our initial viability but still we couldn't get the funders to move. Patience, persistence and endurance were called for.

Month 12: major contracts confirmed

- ☐ second major contract confirmed
- ☐ third major contract confirmed
- ☐ start pressurising funders for decisions
- ☐ zero in on smallest of funding sources
- ☐ £5,000 'booster' loan approved.

Continued prospecting, appointment making and face-to-face selling resulted in pulling off another two big deals in the early part of Month 12 which motivated my partner and me to lean heavily on the funding sources. The first breakthrough here was due entirely to persistence.

Month 13: lift off . . .

- ☐ fourth major contract confirmed
- ☐ £20,000 of 'soft' loans approved
- ☐ £18,000 of grants approved
- ☐ overdraft facility confirmed
- ☐ move into new premises
- ☐ increase staffing
- ☐ business lifts off . . .

And so it came to pass . . . but without consistent use of the essential qualities discussed in Chapter 8, I don't think we'd have made it. Heavy stuff, but we got there in the end. If you believe you can do it, you will. It's all down to dogged persistence.

LOOKING TO YOUR FUTURE

Even as you're planning for the initial launch you should still be giving some thought to the future of your enterprise. It's never too early to start.

Profitable day-dreaming

A little creative day-dreaming can yield a rich harvest if you practise it on a regular basis.

An interviewer once asked the jazz musician Duke Ellington to explain the secret behind his prolific songwriting output over 60 years. Duke replied, 'Oh, I dream a lot. I got a million dreams. I've been day-dreaming since the day I was born.' Day-dreaming sharpens our focus on creativity and often accelerates the process to actuality.

Duke Ellington composed his famous *Mood Indigo* in just 15 minutes while his mother was cooking dinner. That was in 1931. *Mood Indigo* is still being played today, recorded and sold in big numbers – not a bad result for a day-dream of over 60 years ago.

Scenario-planning

Few of us will ever be able to use Duke Ellington's facility for turning dreams into reality to such great effect but what we can do is to take our day-dreams and use them for a little scenario planning.

What is scenario planning? We all do it all the time. It's also called the 'What If' game. What if I did this or that? What if I made a radical change to my pricing policy? What if I offered added value to the service I'm providing? What if I revolutionised my marketing programme? What if I decided suddenly to retire and lie in the sun? What if…?

Scenario planning means making a conscious assessment of how your day-dreams could work out in reality. Try it, it's fun.

Expanding your enterprise

There will come a time not too far away when you will start thinking about expansion. It may be expansion on a small scale, or on a grand scale. Whatever, you'll find scenario planning very helpful in determining which way you want to go and when.

Expanding through franchising

Many new business ideas which have traded successfully have eventually expanded dramatically through franchising. Franchising has played a big part in the development of such names as Coca Cola, Hilton Hotels and a host of well known firms in everything from fast food outlets to vehicle service centres. If your idea is simple to operate and could be replicated by suitably trained others throughout the country, you ought to examine the possibility of franchising as the means to future growth. Typically the franchisor develops a brand name backed by national advertising, and sells licences to independent franchisees to offer the service locally. The franchisor gets his profit from a mixture of lump sum payments and royalties or commissions on sales.

Expanding by trading in Europe

If your expansion plans are on a grander scale, find out as much as you can about what it takes to trade successfully in Europe. There couldn't be a better time to investigate than right now.

Right now there is a lot of money available from the European Union to help you get a business footing in the region. It comes in shape of grants and loans for expenditure on matters such as trade visits, research and product development. Investigate now.

The European Small Business Portal (http://ec.europa.eu/small-business/funding-partners-public/finance/index_en.htm) currently states:

'Access to finance is vital in order to start or expand a business, and the EU provides finance for small firms in different forms – grants, loans, and in some cases, guarantees. In addition, the EU funds specific projects. EU funding can be divided into two categories:

- □ direct funding through grants;
- □ indirect funding through national and local intermediaries.'

Expanding internationally

How far you can travel in expanding your markets is only restricted by how far your ambition can travel. Look into the future now – how far do you think it would lead you, if everything went tremendously well?

ACTION POINTS

1. Find out what help is available for breaking into Europe.

2. Take a sheet of paper and jot down how you envisage your venture will have progressed in (a) five years' time, (b) ten years' time. Examine all the positive possibilities: expansion, franchising, overseas trading, selling out or hanging on in. Have some fun with this exercise without letting your imagination run riot. Mix practicality with a touch of wild blue yondering. Put your lists aside for a month or so, allowing osmosis and catharsis to take over. Then look at them again and you'll find yourself improving on your original outlines. Try it, it works.

11
WHY WOMEN EXCEL IN SMALL BUSINESS

In my time (and in an era when it was unfashionable to do so) I frequently promoted women over men into positions of authority and I did so for reasons close to the heart of the small businessman: practicality, commitment, loyalty. For example, women don't ask the same questions as men, questions like 'Which model and size of car do I get?' and 'How about expenses?' Rather they want to know what they will be doing, what responsibilities they will be taking on. They are focused on personal performance to the exclusion of trappings (which is not to imply they don't appreciate the trappings) and this is why women excel in small business. Their scale of priorities is smack on for commercial success.

Although men and women may approach business in a slightly different way, the explosive growth of women-owned businesses over the past decade attests to the success of their 'non-traditional' style.

- ☐ More than half of women business owners (53 per cent) use intuition or right-brain instead of left-brain thinking, which emphasises analysis, the processing of information methodically, and developing procedures. Intuitive processes often allow someone to see opportunities that aren't readily apparent and to know if they are right without the use of reason and analysis.

- ☐ The way in which women business owners make decisions is usually more whole-brained than men's (*ie* it is more evenly distributed between right-brain and left-brain). This allows someone to use creative and analytical processes, a characteristic that is critical for small business management, especially in uncertain situations.

- ☐ Women business owners tend to reflect on decisions, and to weigh options and outcomes before taking action. In addition, women don't hesitate to gather information from business advisors and associates. The advantage here is the shared knowledge that is gathered through interpersonal interactions and liaisons.

- ☐ Women entrepreneurs describe their businesses in family terms and see their business relationships as a network. This personal touch is often what drives employee motivation and productivity. The downside is, however, that they may lack policies and procedures which are clearly stated.

- ☐ Women have the ability to balance different tasks and priorities. In business for themselves or for someone else, the ability to be flexible and adaptable is a distinct advantage these days when everyone is expected to perform many duties.

☐ Women entrepreneurs tend to find satisfaction and success from building relationships with customers and employees, from having control of their own destiny, and from doing something that they consider worthwhile. We all spend the majority of our lives at work. If our work and our personal values are not in alignment, sooner or later we feel conflict. Women entrepreneurs have used this internal conflict as a motivation in order to create the life that they desire.

☐ Entrepreneurs in general are more similar to each other than they are to the working population in general. Compared to the general working population, entrepreneurs tend to be more logical and analytical in the way they make decisions, no matter what their sex.

WOMEN'S VS MEN'S NEEDS

Women business owners view commercial ownership with different concerns and interests than their male counterparts. Although some are interested in a large, profitable organisation, many prefer their new business to be small, friendly and easy to manage. Because growth usually equals structure, many women business owners **choose to remain small** to avoid dealing with an operation that would require layers of management and a culture that might lack support or is rigid, unfriendly, or limiting. They start their businesses for a variety of reasons. Independence, flexibility, freedom from corporate limitations, and the freedom to take risks are usually major motivational factors for the woman who decides to start her own business. In addition, many women seek personal satisfaction, a certain balance, broader horizons, the respect in the industry, the excitement of growth and the opportunity to learn new things. They tend also to set up on their own to create a secure future and to have choices about their lifestyles. Many have a community mission which they plan to support or fund. Many want to provide good jobs and a secure future for a dedicated staff. Finding a better way to deliver services or making a difference in the lives of many people is often at the top of the list.

Measuring success

If you measure success strictly by your business's profitability, it is often difficult to stay focused. However, if success is measured by the journey, and not just with statistics, the path becomes much clearer and easier to follow. By maintaining their freedom and flexibility, women business owners can become truly creative and confident. And by providing an environment that cultivates respectful relationships, owners are able to focus on performance and profitability. This is not easy, but, for women, it is essential and the rewards are definitely worth the effort.

Women opting to be their own boss

Women are voting with their feet and setting up their own businesses to get more flexibility between work and family life, according to a 2008 survey of female entrepreneurs commissioned by the then Minister for Women and Equality, Harriet Harman.

The biggest motivation for going it alone – 70% of those polled – was to be able to work more flexibly, with three quarters (75%) saying work–life balance is better when you run your own business, rather than being an employee.

Women entrepreneurs are overwhelmingly positive about the benefits of being self-employed, with nine in ten (86%) happy to set up their own business all over again.

Additional findings from the survey include:

More than three quarters (78%) gained greater independence from setting up their own business, two thirds (66%) increased confidence, and 60% said it gave them greater self-worth.

Other reasons for women starting their own business are to be their own boss (65%), to be able to work from home (61%), to get more job satisfaction (53%), to achieve a better work–life balance (52%).

The proportion of manual/unskilled (C2DE) female entrepreneurs is increasing – 55% set up their business in the past five years, compared with 47% of professional/skilled women (ABC1), indicating that starting up a new business is not just for those with degrees.

Female entrepreneurship in the United Kingdom is increasing. There are now more than one million self-employed women – a 17% rise since 2000. But the gap between female and male entrepreneurship remains stubbornly wide. Despite women making up half of the UK population, they only constitute 27% of the self-employed.

Ms Harman said at a reception to celebrate women's contribution to the UK economy:

'Women want to call the shots by running their own business. They're recognising that being their own boss gives them control and allows them to balance their work and family life. Mothers often tear their hair out trying to balance earning a living with bringing up their children, and need more flexibility from their work. Setting up their own business can be the solution.

But we need to encourage more women to take the plunge. Men are almost twice as likely as women to start a new business. That's why we are determined to close this gap by providing solid support and encouragement.'

At the reception Business Secretary of State John Hutton said:

'Increasing entrepreneurship among the UK's women brings us huge economic benefits – maximising an untapped economic dividend and increasing productivity.

If the UK matched the USA's level of women-led businesses we would have an additional 900,000 businesses and 150,000 start-ups every year. I want us to be the most enterprising economy in the world and to do this, we need women to start and grow their own businesses. That's why measures to boost female entrepreneurships are central to our recent enterprise strategy.'

The Government recently announced an Enterprise Strategy, with measures to increase the number of women's entrepreneurs, including a £12.5 million Women's Investment Fund with the aim of private sector to match the funding to develop women-led businesses. Other measures include a pilot of US-model Women's Business Centres and the establishment of a national mentoring network, both of which will provide women entrepreneurs with support and advice.

Advice and support on setting up in business is available from local Business Link offices or http://www.businesslink.gov.uk/

 Here's a website whose sole aim is to aid women in business in the UK with networking, marketing, promoting and information. You can also list your business for free in one business category *http://www.onewoman business.co.uk.*

Contrasting statistics from the USA

There are exciting things happening inside the world of women entrepreneurs. Women are now the dominant force in small business ownership, and succeeding in industries that were once taboo for women.

By studying industries, sales trends, and other important statistics, you can make better business decisions now, and viable plans for future growth.

Women are not only starting businesses, they are staying in business

Between 1997 and 2006, businesses fully women-owned, or majority-owned by women, grew at nearly twice the rate of all U.S. firms (42.3% vs. 23.3%). During this same time period, employment among women-owned firms grew 0.4%, and annual sales grew 4.4%.

In 2006, reports on women-owned (or majority owned by women) in the United States returned the following impressive statistics:

- ☐ There were an estimated 10.4 million privately-held firms;
- ☐ This accounted for two in five (40.2%) of all businesses in the country; and
- ☐ These firms generated $1.9 trillion in annual sales and employed 12.8 million people nationwide.

THE VALUE OF PERSONAL GOAL-SETTING

Personal goal-setting is crucial when you are deciding whether or not you would like to own your own business. Because your business will have an impact on every other area of your existence, it is critical to know how it fits into your lifestyle and whether it allows you to reach your other goals. Two of the benefits you will receive as a result of defining and aligning your major goals in life are **peace of mind** and **focus**. Let us take a look at a few of the other benefits of personal goal-setting:

□ Know, be, do and have more.
□ Use your mind and talents fully.
□ Have more purpose and direction in life.
□ Make better decisions.
□ Be more organised and effective.
□ Do more for yourself and others.
□ Have greater confidence and self-worth.
□ Feel more fulfilled.
□ Be more enthusiastic and motivated.
□ Accomplish uncommon projects.

Remember, you will not pay a price for setting goals. You will pay a price for **not** setting them. We can choose to get caught up in the everyday activity of our lives without feeling any real sense of purpose or we can choose to accomplish something meaningful with our lives that gives us a sense of direction and self-motivation.

> **Ninety-seven per cent of the population does not set goals for two major reasons: (1) FEAR (False Evidence Appearing Real) is preventing them from doing so and (2) there is a risk that the goal may not be reached.**

One question a lot of women ask is how to know if a goal is good or bad. In other words, how do you discriminate between the really important goals and the nice-to-have but not really important ones? You will know whether or not a goal you have chosen is important by answering these five questions.

□ Is it really my goal?
□ Is it morally right and fair?
□ Are my short-range goals consistent with my long-term goals?
□ Can I commit myself emotionally to completing the project?
□ Can I visualise myself reaching this goal?

If you have answered 'no' to even one of these questions, you may want to reconsider this goal. In the short term it may appear to work for you, but in the long run, you may exposing yourself to a lot of unnecessary conflict and frustration. Be sure to set big goals as well as multiple goals. Big goals force you to reach in and use the potential that is inside of you. Long-range goals help you to overcome short-range failures. They can also help you to change your direction without going back on your decision. Whether or not they ever reach the goals they have set, people who set big, long-range goals have been found to have higher self-confidence, higher self-esteem, and greater personal motivation. The bottom line is that more than half the rewards and benefits achieved from goal-setting come from actually taking your first step in that direction, regardless of the consequences.

There is a very simple process in seven steps that you can go through to set any goal whether personal or professional. To be effective, the goal you choose must include all seven of the following steps:

1. Identify your goal by writing it down.
2. Set a deadline for the achievement. Put a date on it.
3. List the obstacles to overcome in accomplishing your goal.
4. Identify the people and groups you need to work with to reach your goal.
5. List the skills and knowledge required to reach your goal. (What do you need to know?)
6. Develop a plan of action to reach your goal.
7. Write down the benefits of achieving your goal. (What is in it for me?)

Alarm Bell

Do this now. Provide answers to questions (1) to (5); then expand on an action plan for achieving your goals together with a list of the benefits accruing thereto.

On a periodic basis, it is important to re-evaluate your goals to make certain that they are in alignment with what you truly value and want out of life. Remember, goal-setting is a life-long process. Once you have completed one goal, be sure to replace it with something else. This way you will always reap the benefits that goal-setting provides.

DECIDING THE RIGHT TIME TO START UP ON YOUR OWN

Overall, specialists who study small business start-ups have found that the most important characteristics for success include:

□ Knowledge in the field through both formal training and on-the-job experience.
□ Attitude or willingness to work long hours for many months and sometimes years, without expecting much income.
□ A business plan – a business without a plan is like a ship without a rudder.
□ Capital, cash, resources.
□ Action – implementation – get-it-done.

If you are at the point where you feel comfortable with these five areas, there is a very high probability that you will succeed should you decide to start your own business. However, if you feel weak in one or more of these areas, you may want to ask yourself if 'now' really is the right time.

The personal resources you will require to commit

Being self-employed usually requires more knowledge, time, planning, resources, and energy than working for someone else. Make sure that you are willing and able to commit to whatever it takes to make your venture a success. This may mean taking into consideration any other goals that you may have, as well as current and future responsibilities. As a general rule, estimate the amount of time you think you'll spend on your business and double it. Believe it or not, this is one of the best ways to determine the time commitment that you will be making to run your new business.

Flexibility in application

Obviously, some types of businesses are more flexible in terms of time commitment than others. You might want to adjust your business goals to meet your lifestyle goals. How hard do you want to work? Do you want to hustle sales every day? If you are determined that your weekends are free, you should eliminate retail sales, real estate, and many service businesses from your list of possibilities. But you shouldn't get discouraged. There are businesses to match every lifestyle and you have to find one that is right for you. Be sure to involve your family in the decision process. Their support is critical. They will help you narrow your search and they can also be your supporters as you climb the mountain.

NARROWING THE FOCUS TO MEET YOUR OBJECTIVES

There are thousands of different types of businesses in the marketplace. Each business fills a certain need that the market is demanding. In some ways, this is good because it gives you unlimited choices for the type of business you can start. On the other hand, it may be overwhelming to try to sift through all of the different possibilities and choose the right one for you. In order to make this process easier, here is a step-by-step procedure for narrowing your business options. **First, let's start with you**. Your search for the right business idea will be aided by learning the necessary steps to take so you can best assess your interests, skills, abilities, knowledge, and talents. Once you have determined what you are interested in and skilled at, we can take a look at the marketplace to see what is being demanded by the consumer.

A personal assessment for determining your business idea

Basic ideas for your business most often come from the following sources:

- ☐ As spin-off from your present occupation.
- ☐ A hobby or special interest.
- ☐ An answer to the question, 'Why isn't there a . . .?'
- ☐ A shortcoming in the products or services of others.
- ☐ New or different way of using ordinary things.
- ☐ An observed need.
- ☐ Technological advance or changes in society or social custom.

To help in your search for the right idea, take the following steps and assess your interests, skills, abilities, knowledge and talents to help you determine what you are best at.

Part 1. Assess your interests

Your interests are simply your likes and dislikes, your preference for one thing and your dislike of another. Begin by writing down what interests you. Start with broad categories.

- ☐ What are your hobbies currently? What were they when you were younger?
- ☐ What school courses did you enjoy when you were younger?
- ☐ Were there any jobs that you really liked or got a lot of satisfaction from?

□ What kind of sports and recreational activities have you participated in and enjoyed?

□ What do you do in your spare time? What would you like to do if you could?

□ What do you consider to be a lot of fun?

Once you have created your list of interests, identify anything that you particularly dislike doing. List these activities below your interests along with the reasons for your dislike. Your interest inventory is not a rigid indicator of what you should do. It is only a starting point for helping you learn the range of your interests. It is important not to confuse interests with abilities and skills. Once you have completed this list, review the activities and interests you have identified and look for patterns. Do any appear consistently? If so, circle them.

Part 2. Building your skills inventory

The key to picking your business idea is knowing and being able to articulate all the different skills you possess. The word 'skills' is being used in the most general sense possible. You are not looking for skills which you and you alone possess in all the world. It is sufficient that you have the skill to any degree. You are looking for any you may have exhibited while doing something. You will need to really open yourself up when making your list. After you have developed your list, circle those skills which represent your strongest abilities and which you take the greatest pleasure in performing. Now see whether a pattern exists that can lead you to explore what your business should be. Write down any patterns that appear.

Part 3. Recalling your 'power stories'

Everyone has memories of times in their lives when they felt particularly strong and on track. It may be the time you gave your first speech, or the day your child was born, or it may be the time you reached a goal you had previously thought impossible. Whatever it is, these are the times when you felt the most proud of yourself. Call these memories 'power stories'. Whether or not anyone else is aware of these times in your life or thinks they are important is irrelevant. The important thing is that they matter to you. Recall a list of seven personal power stories. Divide a sheet of paper in half. On the left side of the page, write down each of your power stories. On the right side, list the skills and talents you used in each story. What skills and talents reappear in each story? Circle those.

Part 4. Building your special knowledge inventory

List any special knowledge you have acquired according to the following sources:

□ Learned in school or college.

□ Learned on the job or by actually doing at home or work.

□ Learned from seminars or workshops.

□ Learned by reading avidly.

□ Learned by talking to people.

You should list as many special types of knowledge as you can think of. Circle the five types that you would like to use in business.

Part 5. Self-estimates

On a scale of 1 (low) to 7 (high), rate yourself (as compared with other people) on each of the following traits. Be as objective and accurate as possible. Remember, there are no right or wrong answers. Try not to rate yourself the same in each ability.

_____ Clerical	_____ Musical	_____ Teaching
_____ Managerial	_____ Technical	_____ Scientific
_____ Mechanical	_____ Empathic	_____ Building
_____ Numerical	_____ Sales	_____ Artistic

Then list your top four traits with the rating for each.

Part 6. Dividing up your time

You need to decide, as a future business owner, how you want your time to be spent. Divide the following categories in terms of percentages of time per week based on 100 per cent. Try not to give each one the same percentage.

☐ With people:
☐ With information:
☐ With things:

Part 7. Why do you want to start your own business?

Write down all the reasons why you want to start your own business.

Part 8. Determining your priorities

As you begin combining your work and family responsibilities, make sure you know what your priorities are. Begin by listing any current time commitments and then estimate how much time you spend on these regular activities. Think through your priorities. What activities must you continue? What can you let others do? What activities are expendable? Now that you have completed your personal assessment for helping to determine your business idea, try to pull the information together to see whether a picture of yourself has emerged so that you can gain a sense of what type of business would best suit your skills, knowledge, business goals, and your reasons for wanting to start a business. You most likely will begin to see a pattern that leads to a specific idea or to a general category of business such as service, retail, or manufacturing.

MATCHING PERSONAL INTERESTS WITH MARKETPLACE NEEDS

Research indicates more and more that you must enjoy what you are doing if you want to be successful in the long run. If you start a business based on the latest get-rich quick scheme, you will find yourself getting tired very quickly. On the other hand, if you focus only on what you like and you disregard the needs of the marketplace, you may soon find yourself scraping to pay your bills at the end of the month. Then what is the answer? Like most of the things in life, the answer is to find a balance. It is likely that almost anything you would like to give, someone else in the world would like to receive. The trick is to find that person and present your product or your service in such a way that they simply can't resist what you have to offer. This is matching personal interests with marketplace needs.

Let's look at an example...

Susan was very interested in adventure travel. She had worked as a travel agent for several years and she was now thinking about starting an adventure travel company for women. She decided to test the waters by putting an advertisement in *Cosmopolitan*. When very few people responded to her ad, she became very disillusioned and decided that her idea might never be successful. That's when a friend told her of a new magazine that she had just seen at the news stand called *Outside Woman*. It sounded interesting so she purchased the magazine and read it. After talking to the editor of the magazine, she learned that a lot of women who read this particular magazine were interested in travel as a way to open their worlds and go beyond their fears. Susan also learned that most of these women were in their 30s and 40s, not early 20s as she had previously thought. Armed with this new knowledge, she created an adventure package that aimed at 'women who wanted to experience the spiritual side of adventure travel' and she placed an ad in the magazine that her friend had recommended. The response was tremendous. Within several weeks, she was able to book a first group outing and her business was born. Susan's story is one of success. However, without a little luck, her story could have been one of failure. Market research is often the difference between succeeding and failing miserably. Susan never gave up her dream of doing something she loved. But until she reached the right group in the marketplace, she was doomed to failure. **Moral of the story?** Look inside yourself to learn what you like and what your dreams are. Then open your eyes and take the time to find others with whom you could share your dream. All in all, it may take you a little longer, but it will be worthwhile.

VISUALISING YOURSELF IN BUSINESS

When you are trying to choose the best business for yourself, it is easy to get caught up in the belief that what you have been doing, you must continue to do. Without careful consideration, you may end up trading your small office or cubicle at work for a small room at home that keeps you just as tied down as your old job. Or you may end up having to spend most of your day pounding the pavement on sales calls when what you really wanted was to remain at home for most of the day. To help you 'feel' your business before you start it, you may want to try using visualisation to get a mental picture of what your day will be like. By doing this, you will discover what you will be feeling as you go through a typical business day. You can then use this information to help you determine if you are on the right professional track.

Before you invest money, time and energy

It's important to evaluate the lifestyle of your business direction before investing money, time and energy in it. Going into business for the wrong reasons (*ie* a panic decision to quit an undesirable job, impulsively starting a business just because, or simply to have more time) without adequate research can be a ticket to failure, either in your professional life, your personal life, or both.

Questionnaire to get you thinking

The following questions are a simple way to get you thinking about what your day will look like once you own your business. As you consider each question, notice how you feel. Do you feel tense and agitated as you read each question or are you getting excited and motivated? Even if you don't know the reason why, listen to your feelings and trust yourself.

1. It's time to get ready for your business day. What time is it?

2. You get dressed for work. What do you wear?

3. Someone depends on you before you leave. Who is it? What do they need?

4. You open your door to your business. Where is it located? What does it look like?

5. You look around. Who else is there with you?

6. You produce (or handle) the product of your business. What is it?

7. A customer purchases that product. What does he/she look like? Male? Female? Age? Occupation?

8. You've started building customers. Why did the customer choose your product/service and how did he/she know about it?

9. You think about your product or service. What does it cost? How did the customer pay for it? Cash? Credit card? On account?

10. You glance down at your customer list. What and when will he/she purchase from you the next time?

11. It's lunch/dinner time. What are you eating?

12. You eat. Where? With whom?

13. The morning has come and gone. What do you see yourself doing during the second half of your day. Producing something? Selling something? Going somewhere?

14. It's time to close up. What time is it?

15. You prepare your bills or count your money. How much did you 'make' today? How much is in actual cash? How much is owed to you?

16. It's time to go home. Are you going straight home or do you have to stop somewhere first?

17. You've arrived home. Do you have household responsibilities when you get home?

18. You need to do book/paper work for your business. When do you do it?

19. You want to talk about your day with someone. Who do you talk to?

20. You prepare for your business for the next day. What do you do?

21. It's time to sleep. What time is it?

APPRECIATING YOUR SELF-WORTH

Self-esteem and self-confidence are essential to the health and well-being of every person. If you are thinking of starting your own business, you must know and trust in the fact that you are capable of facing and overcoming any challenges that await you. Without such belief, success will be extremely difficult, if not impossible, for you to achieve. If you do not believe in yourself or your product, you will project an air of defeat which others will sense. The end result is that no one will feel comfortable buying from your business.

What is self-esteem?
- ☐ Appreciating one's own worth and importance and having the character to be accountable for oneself and to act responsibly toward others.
- ☐ Confidence and satisfaction in oneself.
- ☐ An absolute necessity.

To better understand yourself and to identify whether or not you may be lacking in self-esteem, review the list of items below. Check off the characteristics in the list that you think apply to you. It's important that you be as honest with yourself as you can.

1. Constantly put myself down; am highly self-critical ☐

2. Have difficulty accepting compliments ☐

3. Often feel victimised by others ☐

4. Feel lonely, even when with other people ☐

5. Feel empty – like I have a hole inside ☐

6. Feel different from other people ☐

7. Feel depressed ☐

8. Feel shame and guilt ☐

9. Don't believe in my own ability; have self-doubts ☐

10. Fear new situations ☐

11. Fear failure ☐

12. Fear success ☐

13. Fear being out of control ☐

14. Have high need to please others ☐

15. Anxious in business settings (panic attacks, anxiety) ☐

16. Managing time demands; feel stress, excessive worry ☐

17. Put things off and get into trouble for it ☐

18. Vulnerable to others' criticism, real or imagined ☐

19. Don't state opinions for fear of what others will think ☐

20. Keep others at a distance emotionally ☐

21. Have self-destructive behaviours ☐

22. 'Numb out' to relax (watch TV, eat, sleep, fantasise) ☐

23. Have negative attitudes; use negative self-talk ☐

24. Have difficulty setting and sticking to goals ☐

25. Have trouble asking for what I want and need ☐

26. Am often angry and aggressive ☐

27. Make unrealistic self-assessments ☐

28. Think in black or white; no tolerance for ambiguity ☐

29. Can't tolerate imperfection ☐

30. Don't feel connected to family or community ☐

31. Lack pride in or information about my ethnic, cultural, or gender group ☐

Once you have identified all of the characteristics that apply to you, go back over this list and pick four areas you see as most vital to the success of your business. Think about each of them. Brainstorm ways in which you could improve these four areas of your life. Set solution-based goals and then track them so that you can see your progress.

WOMEN OPTING TO BE THEIR OWN BOSS

Women-owned businesses generate about $3 trillion in revenue and employ 16% of the workforce, making them significant players in the national economy, according to a recent benchmark study.

The study was led by the non-profit Center for Women's Business Research with sponsorship from Women Impacting Public Policy, a non-partisan group, and Wal-Mart, the world's largest retailer. The research provided an in-depth look at the economic impact of women-owned businesses, which were defined as privately held companies at which women held at least a 50% stake. According to the study, those businesses employ 23 million people, nearly double the number of the 50 biggest companies in the country combined.

Advocates for women in business said the results are a wake-up call for those who consider women to be niche players.

This really gives us good, secure statistics to go to policymakers with,' said Margaret Barton, executive director of the National Women's Business Council.

The study was released during the Economic Summit for Women Business Owners. Among the top issues for members were access to capital for small businesses, the impact of the government's stimulus programs and the cost of health care.

Marion Bonhomme owns Knowledge Connections, a telecommunications engineering and consulting firm based in Herndon. She said her main concern was securing financing. Her bank reduced her line of credit and increased interest rates and fees in the wake of the credit crunch, she said. That has forced her to lay off 10% of her more than 100 employees.

'I could not get the financing in order to support them,' she said.

Bonhomme said she hoped that attending the summit would allow her voice – and those of other women business owners – to be heard.

THE PROS AND CONS OF WORKING AT HOME

With today's rising demand for service-oriented businesses along with recent technological advances, the opportunities for home-based businesses have never been better. However, before taking the plunge, you may want to consider some of the pros and cons of working from home.

The PROS of a home-based business include:

☐ **Financial benefits**. One of the biggest advantages of a home-based business is the financial benefits it provides. A home-based business allows you to eliminate the cost of an office, a major expense for most small businesses. Also, most home-based business owners are eligible for a partial write-off of their house payment, utilities, and maintenance costs. (The laws are becoming stricter in this area. Be sure to check the current tax legislation.)

☐ **Flexibility and freedom**. Let's face it. Work takes up a lot of our lives. Because of this, more and more women want the flexibility and freedom associated with owning a small business. Even if they must put in more hours than their corporate counterparts (which is highly unlikely these days), home-based business owners gain the flexibility to structure their own time and control their own lives.

The CONS of a home-based business include:

☐ **Vague boundaries**. One of the greatest challenges of working from home is to set definite boundaries between work and family obligations. Friends and family members may have a difficult time adjusting to the fact that you have to work while you are home. Remember, this is a transition period for them, too. As long as you are straightforward about your expectations, you should be able to eliminate most of the conflicts before they occur.

☐ **Increased self-discipline and isolation**. In addition to the skills every woman needs for starting her own business, a woman who starts her own home-based business must also possess two additional skills – namely, the ability to be self-disciplined and the ability to deal with isolation. These are critical skills for anyone thinking about starting a home-based business. Although you will still have some interaction with the outside world, the chances are it will be far less than you are used to. Be honest with yourself. If the thought of spending many hours alone makes you nauseous or you are easily distracted and find it difficult to complete a project on your own, a home-based business is probably not for you.

A MAJOR FORCE IN WORLD ECONOMICS

Women are not just becoming a major force in the world economy, they already are. Employment by large corporations is generally decreasing but employment by women-owned businesses is growing. In fact, women-owned businesses now are employing 35 per cent more people in the US than the companies in Fortune 500 are employing worldwide. Women business owners are the swashbucklers of this generation. They typically do not inherit family businesses and do not buy established businesses. More likely they start their own businesses because of personal necessity or the lack of opportunity or possibility in the traditional job market. They often start businesses to solve problems that are faced by women and that the marketplace has failed to address, especially in areas of health, child care, education, and fashion.

Women-owned businesses are generally smaller, sleeker, faster and more efficient than their predecessors. There are studies that show that it is more likely for them to offer flexi-time, tuition reimbursement, and job-sharing than US businesses generally offer. Women are addressing problems that have traditionally held women back in the marketplace. All in all, women-owned businesses have become a force that society will require to reckon with.

CASE STUDY

Success in the face of adversity

Penny Ferguson is one woman who is an inspiration to us all. Here she tells her personal success story.

'After facing many personal challenges in my life – being left by my mother as a baby, three traumatic marriages and the devastating loss of my 26-year-old son Phillip, I came to a point in my life where I really didn't know what I wanted to do. I felt battered by life's blows, low in energy and emotionally lost.

I threw myself into various training programmes. In the course of one year I qualified in massage, sports massage, aromatherapy, colour healing, Reiki healing and as a hypnotherapist, probably to heal me as much as anything. I also did a tremendous amount of personal development workshops.

These workshops fascinated me in one respect – there were many business people, some of whom were senior in their organisation, who were very committed to this type of development, but none of them, when I asked them, could think of any way that they used what they learned in the workplace. It was as though this was something that was for them only to be practised at evenings and weekends but not to be talked about back in the workplace – people would think it was all too "pink and fluffy". This really challenged my thinking because I could not see how each person being personally developed did not apply to the whole person – surely it is the same person at home and at work, simply different aspects of the life but the whole person needed to be in both places.

The more I developed these thoughts and developed myself and my thinking I realised that to enable people to become the best they can be it had to be an integral part of their whole life – my vision became clear from that moment on. I also now knew that all my life experiences would help me in being able to work with others – I had been there, got so many things "wrong" in my life, and through changing my thinking could turn it round. I also knew that I could combine personal development with all I knew and had taught in business so that the "soft" side of personal development could be grounded in hard nosed business facts. I felt sure that this could make the teaching of skills come alive in a totally different and more fulfilling way.

I started to work on constructing my own workshop, a course which would help others, not just in their professional lives but their personal lives too – real-life skills. I started my first course with a small group of people in my drawing room. To my surprise, I quickly began to attract more and more interest in my work, just through word of mouth.

Within a year my bank manager was offering me a loan to expand my business. I found it hard to believe my own success. Soon I was taking clients from multi-national companies such as ICI, police forces, the Ministry of Defence, Sun Microsystems, Powergen and Barclays. Many people were wanting to know the secret of my three-day programmes. All I could tell them was that I had combined what I had learnt from my own personal experience with the business skills that I had acquired in management.

What I had come up with was a formula for taking personal development into the business world that was working and people were making significant changes in their lives. That was seven years ago. We have now had over four thousand people who have come through the courses. I act as a private coach to executives internationally, and do public speaking internationally. It is incredibly exciting seeing how many people are changing their lives really significantly and becoming more effective leaders as a result of this work. I also have trained others how to run my programme and I have worked with several big organisations, one being a police force, taking the programme throughout their entire workforce. The feedback from delegates is quite astonishing and clients report significant improvement in bottom line results.

My dream is also to take this into schools and work with young people. On all my workshops I offer one free place to a teacher from a primary or secondary school – it is my way of giving something back and some of the stories I am now being told about the results from teachers who have attended the programme are unbelievably exciting. I am now much clearer about what it is that we are teaching that enables individuals to change their lives, in some instances quite dramatically. It never ceases to amaze me the courage people show in turning their lives around, in some cases, dramatically. I believe that I have used what life has taught me and turned all the negatives into powerful learning experiences.'

If you would like more details please contact Penny Ferguson Limited on 01455 231990 or email: *penny@pennyferguson.com* or visit her website *http://www.pennyferguson.com/*

12

WHY YOU NEED A WEBSITE EVEN IF YOUR BUSINESS IS OFFLINE

You do business offline and you're doing very nicely but you still need a website. Why? Because if you choose to ignore the potential of online trading, you are also choosing to miss out on a valuable extension to your existing customer base. What's more, you are also missing out on the opportunity of getting closer to your current clientele. You might think that the net, more specifically your own website, offers few opportunities for businesses with a customer base clustered in a small geographic area. After all, the web is world wide ... a global medium. And you would have been fairly correct up until recently. But matters have been changing rapidly. More and more, *your* potential clients are forsaking those heavy *Yellow Pages* paper books for Google and other engines. It's easier and faster to do a search when you need to find a local supplier in a hurry.

USING THE INTERNET FOR THE PURPOSE IT WAS INVENTED

Use it initially for the purpose for which it was invented. Use it as a channel of information.

1. A channel for receivable information.
2. A channel for deliverable information.

Doing it this way provides you with two valuable operational devices. The facility to receive information opens the door to ongoing market research while the facility to deliver information electronically presents you with a cyberspace marketing application. Using the internet search facilities, you can keep tabs on your competition. You can source valuable applications and software – and all for free. You can be on constant lookout for new ideas. Using the net as a marketing application, you can create a powerful website:

1. To promote your product or service.
2. To foster loyalty with existing customers.
3. To service their requirements.
4. To answer prospects' questions.
5. To pre-sell prospective customers before they call on you.
6. To provide them with additional information.
7. To attract new customers.
8. To capture email addresses to build lists of potential customers.
9. To keep tabs on competitors.
10. To raise your profile above that of the competition.

You can do all of this – and if you go about matters in the right way, you can achieve your objective on a limited budget.

Consider this: perhaps your product or service already has the propensity for transference into a digital format; perhaps too its potential distribution is not as localised as you think. Stick with it and as the retail ethos of the internet continues to intensify will do more and more business in time.

WHY THE INTERNET IS SUCH A WONDERFUL MARKETING TOOL

We all know the web is a resource for fun and information. Have you ever stopped to really think about why it's such a wonderful marketing tool? If you already use a website to market your business, or are considering doing so, the following concepts may give you something new to consider.

1. A website is a fun and creative way to express yourself

The idea of online marketing seems to make many of us a bit uncomfortable. Using a website as a marketing tool is a way of hanging up your virtual shingle, where you can really have fun and get creative in the process.

2. Anyone can have a website

Financially speaking, the web is 'The Great Equaliser' of the marketing world. Whereas other forms of advertising and marketing, such as television, radio, and print media, are often prohibitively expensive for small companies or individuals, anyone can use the web to advertise and market their products or services for approximately the same reasonable rates. While the cost of creating a website may vary (based on size, the nature and amount of graphic design used, and the experience level of the designer), the cost of running or maintaining a website over time is minimal as compared with other media. It is a means of advertising that is financially within reach of everyone.

3. Your website is a direct reflection of *you*

As the owner of your own website, you control the message and image you want to portray. You get to decide what you want to say with it – it's your own personal billboard. You have as much space to get your message across as you need, so use it well. Make it attractive, professional and functional, make it well organised. Be sure the real *you* comes through on the screen. Imagine you are a potential client visiting your site for the first time – as a new client, what are you looking for? How easy it is to find pertinent information about you and your business? What's in it for the client – why should they not only do business with you, but repeatedly visit your site to enhance their experience of your product or services?

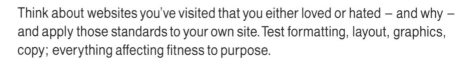

Alarm Bell
Think about websites you've visited that you either loved or hated – and why – and apply those standards to your own site. Test formatting, layout, graphics, copy; everything affecting fitness to purpose.

4. **This is one time where it's considered OK to be a 'work in progress'**
With the web, you're virtually unlimited (pun intended). You can change it as often as you see fit – and frequent website updates are in fact highly desirable. The more fresh and innovative the content, the more valuable it will be to others. It is critical that you periodically review your site to see if it's getting stale and outdated, and that you use your website to keep your target market informed.

Alarm Bell

Even if your site is more or less under construction, dump those 'under construction' messages or graphics – a good site is always a work in progress, and using those messages marks you as an amateur.

5. **You'll have room to experiment freely – the web is a very forgiving medium of self-expression**
The great thing about the web is that by its very nature, it is intended to be changeable and flexible. Don't worry about getting it perfect or that you are locked into a design or look.

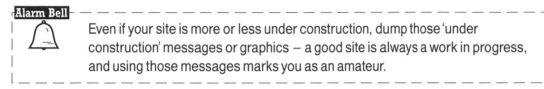

It's handy to have everything you need to know about websites in one place. Email *jimgreen@writing-for-profit.com* with WEBSITE HANDBOOK in the subject line and I'll send you a PDF of this instructive manual.

THE BEST WAY TO CREATE A DEDICATED WEBSITE

What you need to make the most of the e-commerce experience is composite software that frees up time to enable you to concentrate on the primary function: marketing the business. Such all-embracing software is available to you and it is proving a popular route with many business owners because it is less demanding and permits one-to-one interfacing with potential customers. Should this be of interest to you (and it's worth investigating) you might consider investing in the all-in-one tool that I use. It will set you back around £274 per annum but what you receive for your money is awesome. **Site Build It!** is available for immediate download (http://buildit.sitesell.com/interactive1.html) and includes:

- □ domain name registration
- □ hosting
- □ power keyword research, analysis and implementation
- □ graphic tools
- □ point-and-click page building
- □ choice of page templates
- □ FTP
- □ form builder/autoresponder
- □ data transfer
- □ email
- □ newsletter publishing facility

- brainstorming and researching
- spam check
- daily traffic stats and click analysis
- search engine optimisation
- automatic search engine submission
- automatic search engine tracking
- automatic search engine ranking
- pay-per-click research and mass-bidding
- four traffic headquarters
- action guide and fast track guide
- integrated online help
- express ezine to keep you up to date on new developments
- tips and techniques
- customer support
- facility for uploading/downloading digitised data.

Here is an example of a multi-page website I created using Site Build It! http://www.writing-for-profit.com

The Third Sphere alternative

With Third Sphere you get all of the above, plus:

- choice of fonts
- context-sensitive menus when building
- CGI bin
- CGI scripts library
- uploading to server
- password protected pages
- custom error pages
- back-up system
- source code editing
- spell check
- spam blockers
- total marketing automation
- traffic center plus tools
- upload files without FTP
- edit HTML on screen
- anti-virus software
- secure space (product delivery)
- PDF ebook creator (ex-Word files).

On the face of it (at £14 per month) this looks like the better bet and that is why I intend to try it out myself on some test marketing – but there's a 'but' and it's a big 'but' – the **Third**

Sphere Traffic Center does not appear to have anything like the power of **Site Build It!** This could result in traffic optimisation being left entirely to your own devices which could in the long run prove very costly.

Here are 5 samples from a series of mini websites I recently constructed using **Third Sphere** on a trial basis but whether they will all still be functioning by the time you read this will depend upon how I assess performance of the system during the test run.

http://start-a-business-masterplan.com
http://1st-creative-writing-course.com
http://1st-creative-writing-course.com/gettingpublished.html
http://1st-creative-writing-course.com/makemoney.html
http://retirement-moneymakers.com

Alternatively, you could opt for a free page building and hosting service – but that's all you'll get. If you do, choose the best – www.freeservers.com.

 To enhance your presence online you can submit your website to 473 web directories. Send a blank email to *jimgreen@writing-for-profit.com* with DIRECTORY 2 in the subject line and I'll send you a PDF listing all 473 directories.

UNSPOKEN SECRETS

And finally, here are nine 'unspoken secrets' to ensure success for your online marketing . . .

Unspoken Secret 1: People want stuff that is automatic, where you do it ALL for them, and they don't have to do a thing. Create all your products with this in mind, and they're virtually guaranteed to sell like hotcakes.

Unspoken Secret 2: There is *always* an easier, better, quicker, more effective and profitable way to do everything you're doing right now. Go find it!

Unspoken Secret 3: *Thinking* that you are 'successful' can lull you into a sense of false security and make you lose your razor-sharp edge, which was responsible for your success in the first place.

Unspoken Secret 4: Forget about waiting to be 'inspired'. Motion beats meditation. Force yourself to do ANYTHING that brings you a step closer to your goals.

Unspoken Secret 5: 'The very essence of all power to influence lies in getting the other person to participate. The mind that can do that has a powerful leverage on his human world.' – Harry A. Overstreet

Unspoken Secret 6: Never be afraid to raise your prices if you are convinced that your produce is commensurate with the value you place on it. Nobody would want caviar if it were cheap.

Unspoken Secret 7: Internet marketing is like chess. You spend your time learning all you can about the various moves and how each one relates to another. You think about nothing else but 'winning' and you're always many moves ahead of the competition.

Unspoken Secret 8: Possessing an intimate knowledge of your market is far more important than knowing any of the so-called new fangled marketing ideas.

Unspoken Secret 9: Never be afraid to take big risks and do BIG things. Anything worth doing, is worth screwing up badly until you finally get it right!

SOCIAL MEDIA: TAILORMADE FOR SMALL BUSINESS

To create a really compelling online presence for your small business you need more than a website; you need to participate in social media activity on a regular basis.

I was using social media for many years before the terms Web 2.0, social marketing and bookmarking became fashionable buzz words. I frequented places where people congregate to:

- exchange views
- offer opinions
- ask questions
- seek or offer assistance
- make friends.

Early on I discovered that social media was an excellent vehicle for maintaining the status I had attained in other directions; not by overt promotion but by giving freely of my expertise and dispensing knowledge gratis.

- **Radio** is social media.
- **Article distribution** is social media.
- **Video channels** are social media.
- **Public speaking** is social media.
- **Book reviewing** is social media.
- **Writing circles** are social media.
- **Forums** are social media.

Nowadays though, the opportunities to engage in social marketing are more and more widespread than ever before; offering a variety of ingenious ways of unobtrusively strutting your stuff before a receptive audience without ever getting in their face or causing offence.

Cashing in on the social networking phenomenon

Let's begin with a basic outline...

Web 2.0 and *social networking* are interchangeable terms that are used to describe interactive environments and communication strategies applied on the internet.

Web 2.0 is a general term applied to any website that reacts to the input and activity of its users, such as a blog, a MySpace profile, a forum, or a Squidoo lens page.

Social networking is best defined as the regular interaction of people for some common cause. Of course there is really nothing new about social networking, and it's something many of us do every day offline, especially in schools or in the workplace. But as a marketing trend this concept is growing more and more popular online.

But first, a few questions that require answers before we proceed further:

- ☐ What is social media?
- ☐ What is social marketing?
- ☐ What is social bookmarking?

Social media allows people with basic computer skills to tell their stories using publishing tools such as blogs, video logs, photo sharing, podcasting (audio stories broadcast from the web or downloaded to a computer) and wikis (collaboratively edited web pages). They can also help us filter and organise the overwhelming amount of information on the web.

Social Media Marketing (SMM) is a form of internet marketing which seeks to achieve branding and marketing communication goals through the participation in various social media networks such as MySpace, Facebook, Bebo, YouTube, Dailymotion, hi5, Gather, and social web applications (webapps) such as reddit, Digg, StumbleUpon, Flickr, iLike, Wikipedia, Squidoo, Last.fm, Twitter, Eventful, ePinions, and many others.

Social bookmarking is a user-defined taxonomy system for bookmarks. Such a taxonomy is sometimes called a folksonomy (*the spontaneous cooperation of a group of people to organise information into categories*) and the bookmarks are referred to as tags. Unlike storing bookmarks in a folder on your computer, tagged pages are stored on the Web and can be accessed from any computer. Technorati, a blogging site, describes the system as "The real-time Web, organised by you". Websites dedicated to social bookmarking, such as Flickr and Delicious, provide users with a place to store, categorise, annotate and share favourite web pages and files.

So what, you might well ask, has any or all of this to do with helping me establish myself as an expert in my niche and proceeding to maintain that status?

A great deal in my experience, providing you treat social networking as an adjunct to online marketing activity and **not** as a replacement; providing too you keep your approach simple and consistent.

DEVISING A ROUTE THAT MEETS YOUR SPECIFIC NEEDS
- ☐ No two people have identical aims in their approach to social marketing.

□ No one knows your niche and marketplace better than you.

Tailor your own route accordingly

1. Choose social sites appropriate to your market.
2. Choose bookmarking link sites to meet your needs.
3. Post information that reflects your marketplace.
4. Create how-to/product review videos in like manner.
5. Set up blogs to drive traffic to your websites.
6. Attract like-minded visitors to your social websites.
7. Feed them regularly with informative snippets.

Don't treat social marketing as a sales tool

Social marketing is not a sales tool per se but it can drive sales in the long term by:

□ enhancing your reputation
□ catapulting your blogs and websites hand-in-hand to top rankings in the major search engines.

To provide you with a feel for the power of social marketing, have a look at this...

1. **Social media giant Facebook** is currently adding a million 25+ (non-student) adults per week to their rosters – that's 52 million new users a year...

2. **YouTube.com** gets over 50 million unique visitors per month – over half a billion a year...

3. **MySpace.com** sees over 49 million unique visitors each month – over 1.6 million a day...

That's a stack of traffic and the social marketing websites (there are 1,500 of them) are currently outstripping Google and Yahoo in visitor attraction.

You can tap into this swarm of ever-growing enthusiasm if you know how – and *you will do* by the time you've finished reading through this instructional nutshell.

This stuff works and I can prove it...

How to make social media work for your business

The good news is it is easy to start the process of using social media to maintain your status as an expert in your niche and here is the formula in sequence:

1. Visit each of the following social media networks in turn and examine the profiles

Facebook *http://facebook.com*
My Space *http://myspace.com*
Squidoo *http://squidoo.com*
Hub Pages *http://hubpages.com*

YouTube *http://youtube.com*
Bebo *http://bebo.com*
Dailymotion *http://dailymotion.com*
hi5 *http://hi5.com*
Gather *http://gather.com*

Sign up for the first five for sure and select one more from the remaining four options.

2. Now visit each of these social bookmarking websites and once again study the profiles

Propellor *http://propeller.com*
Slashdot *http://slashdot.org*
Digg *http://digg.com*
Technorati *http://technorati.com*
Delicious *http://Delicious/*
StumbleUpon *http://stumbleupon.com*
Twitter *http://twitter.com*
reddit *http://reddit.com*
Fark *http://fark.com*
Newsvine *http://newsvine.com*
SWiK *http://swik.net*
Connotea *http://connotea.org*
Sphinn *http://sphinn.com*
BlinkList *http://blinklist.com*
Faves *http://faves.com*
Mister Wong *http://mister-wong.com*
Spurl.net *http://spurl.net*
Netvouz *http://netvouz.com*
Diigo *http://diigo.com*
RawSugar *http://rawsugar.com*
BibSonomy *http://bibsonomy.org*
folkd.com *http://folkd.com*
linkaGoGo *http://linkagogo.com*

Sign up for the first ten and select five more from the remainder.

Creating a compelling presence in social networks

MySpace http://myspace.com is the largest and best-known social network. Individuals create profiles about themselves and then invite similarly minded people to become their online friends. When someone becomes a friend, you can communicate with them and subtly direct them towards your own website.

Setting up your own page is simple and free. Follow the instructions and create your profile by inserting a brief description about yourself and a link to a more detailed biography page on your own website.

Remember, the goal of this page is to drive people to your own site so make sure you get plenty of links included without overtly promoting your website.

Spend an hour every week:

- ☐ developing your channel
- ☐ building your list of friends
- ☐ inviting people to comment.

With your very own MySpace.com page under your belt, do likewise at these core social media concerns:

Facebook
http://facebook.com

Squidoo
http://squidoo.com

Hub Pages
http://hubpages.com

Create a group and an 'event' on Facebook

Facebook is fast catching up on MySpace mainly because of the inventive applications it offers and contrary to popular belief Facebook is **not** an exclusive domain for kids; 37 per cent of the membership is in the 35+ age bracket.

Wait until you have built up your friends base to around 500 and then:

- ☐ start your own group
- ☐ create an event.

Your group will consist of like-minded enthusiasts who will cheerfully flock to your event; an event-cum-group like this...

I have discovered Facebook extremely instrumental in maintaining my own status as a bestselling author and online marketer; *apply yourself* and it will do the same for you.

 Social media is forever evolving and you need to be up to date with changes. Email *jimgreen@writing-for-profit.com* with SM DAILY BLUEPRINT in the subject line and I'll send you a blueprint for marketing your site in social media.

How to use bookmarking links to best advantage

A big part of the social web is the ability for people to build lists of their favourite sites or articles. People with similar interests can then share their lists and benefit from other people's recommendations. If your website has free content, you should make these articles *easy to bookmark* or add to favourites lists. There are a lot of internet sites that now host and share bookmarks. You can add links to these sites to your article pages.

There are two ways of doing this. You can go to each of the leading bookmarking sites and download their code and links onto your site.

The ones that you should include are:

http://digg.com
http://technorati.com
http://delicious
http://reddit.com
http://propeller.com
http://slashdot.org
http://stumbleupon.com
http://twitter.com
http://fark.com
http://newsvine.com

However, if you go down this route it can be time consuming and you will omit many of the potential bookmarking sites. The alternative is to put a link to **http://AddThis.com** on the foot of each page. This gives your users access to over 30 bookmarking sites.

How to ensnare friends and colleagues

Enabling people to easily email an article to a friend is not typically bundled under the heading of social media marketing, but in my view it is another way to encourage people to share and recommend your content. Add an 'Email a Friend' link to all of your content pages.

Why it pays to add a forum

Having a forum on your website is a great way of building a community around your subject area. Monitoring the forum will both give you a chance to understand what people are discussing and promote your expertise by adding your own comments.

The downside of a forum is that it does need to be carefully managed. You need to allow people to make negative comments so they don't feel they are being censored, but you have to stamp out aggressive behaviour, personal insults, spam and meaningless rubbish. This can be time-consuming work, so don't bother with a forum unless you have the time to do it properly.

Non-technical users can pay to use vBulletin http://vbulletin.com. More technical users can use a free open-source solution such as PHPBB http://phpbb.com. To make it easier for people to find you, register your forum with BoardTracker http://boardtracker.com.

Why you don't need a camera to produce videos

It has never been easier to create short videos that can demonstrate your expertise. How-to videos are very popular. For example, if your website is about making money from bric-a-brac, you could create a short video on *How to convert bric-a-brac into hard cash*. Make sure you have your website URL on the opening and closing sequence of your video to promote your website.

Post your videos on YouTube to make it easier for people to find you http://youtube.com and Google Videos http://video.google.com. Give your channel a catchy title and teaser to get people interested. Also link to the videos from your own website.

What's more, you don't need a video camera to become a star

Go to this website and learn how to convert mundane still images into dynamic animated videos *http://moviemakermagic.com*.

If you would like to view examples using still images only, then have a look at any or all of my own how-to videos on YouTube:

http://www.youtube.com/watch?v=tlNZrC3r3tk
http://www.youtube.com/watch?v=8l2YwFQ0OBk
http://www.youtube.com/watch?v=zrSBgioFakI
http://www.youtube.com/watch?v=rl5Wr_ao1GY
http://www.youtube.com/watch?v=TopOGBGAQQo
http://www.youtube.com/watch?v=LmTP8DVy9pk

Why sharing photographs captures visitors

If you have photos related to your subject area, post them on photo sharing websites such as Flikr http://flikr.com and PhotoBucket http://photobucket.com. For example, if your niche is steam trains, take a camera to your next steam train show and post the pictures on these sites. People searching for steam train images are likely to try these sites. They can then follow the link on the photo to your website – but remember to include links back to your own site from the images.

You ought to learn more about social bookmarking than there is space to reveal here. Email *jimgreen@writing-for-profit.com* with BOOKMARK GENERATION 3 in the subject line and I'll send you a comprehensive PDF manual.

Create blogs to drive traffic

Blogs are very simple content sites where short articles are listed one after the other on the home page. They are usually used to write about current events or comment on news.

Some successful content websites are blogs. Some are much more like magazines with feature articles. If your site is more feature-based, consider starting a separate blog that can be more informal and brief. Update the blog every day, even if it is with just one or two-sentence comments. Blogs that are infrequently updated quickly lose their audience.

Using blogs to ensure top ten rakings

You can get basic blogging software for free. Try Wordpress http://wordpress.com or Blogger http://blogger.com. For a managed service, try Typepad http://typepad.com.

I always use Blogger because of its simplicity of operation and despite the sneering cynics, it works well for me. Below is a screen capture of one of the five blogs I created to promote my various interests.

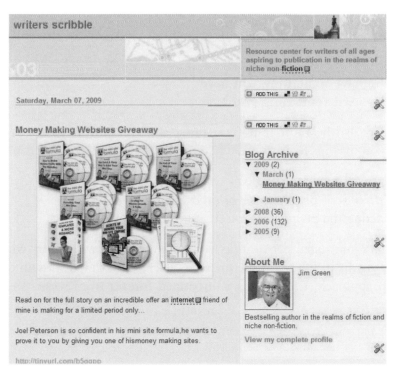

Fig. 4. Example of small business blog.

How social media enhances your reputation

Every week brings more and more evidence of the incredible power of social media websites. Sites like Facebook, MySpace and YouTube drive more and more traffic to websites, generate **multiple front page search engine placements**, and build sales and profits. I can best illustrate this from personal experience.

Observe how applying the social media strategies outlined above has strengthened my overall brand position in the listings of the giant search engines – and in the process:

1. Enhanced my reputation as a creative writing specialist and online marketer.
2. Catapulted my blogs and websites hand-in-hand to top rankings.

WRITING RESIDUALS POWER KIT brand position rankings **1, 3, 4, 5, 6,** 7, **8** on the **first page of 944,800** competitive entries.

ULTIMATE CREATIVE WRITING COURSE brand position rankings **1, 2, 3, 4, 5, 6** in succession on the **first page of 469,900** competitive entries.

WRITERS SCRIBBLE BLOG brand position rankings **1, 2, 3, 4, 5,** 7 on the **first page of 103** competitive entries.

JIM GREEN BOOKMARKS brand position rankings **1, 2, 3, 4, 5,** 7, **8** on the **first page** of 3,850,000 entries.

It won't happen unless you make it happen

What I have achieved in social media marketing in just weeks, so too can you providing you seek out:

- ☐ **people who have something you need**
- ☐ **people who need something you have**.

Whatever your goals, the most important thing is to become involved because nothing happens until you make it happen...

- ☐ Join some social media networks.
- ☐ Read the profiles or profile pages of other members.
- ☐ Start contacting the people who meet your criteria.

Warning: Do *not* join social networking sites with aim of blazing away with your ads to other members via the in-house private message system. Not only is this an extremely lame and amateurish approach, it could get you banned forever from social media marketing participation.

Go social networking, go slowly, go successfully...

SOCIAL MEDIA AND WHY IT'S A PERFECT FIT FOR SMALL BUSINESS

Getting to grips with social media

Here are some sample goals a business owner or manager might set for social media use. Once the goal is considered, then you can look at the tools that are out there and evaluate which ones will give you the best shot of achieving those goals.

20 possible goals

1. I'm a content provider, and I want to expand my reach.
2. I want my customers to be able to stay updated with news about my company.
3. I want to get to know my customers.
4. I want to promote my product.
5. I want to stay abreast of current news and trends.
6. I want to share my ideas with like-minded individuals.
7. I want to increase brand awareness.
8. I want to provide customer service and support easily.
9. I want to find new customers.
10. I want to recruit more staff.
11. I want people to like my brand.
12. I want to collaborate on business projects.
13. I want to directly sell a product.
14. I want to earn respect within my industry.
15. I am getting information overload, and I want to get organised.
16. I want to drive traffic to my site.
17. I want to attract advertisers and make money.
18. I want to get more involved with local prospects.
19. I want to get more involved with people on an international and global level.
20. I want to keep up with my competitors.

There are certainly more possible goals for business social media use out there. I've probably not even scratched the surface. What goals will you set for your social media efforts?

WHY LOCAL SEARCH IS CHANGING AND BECOMING MORE COMPETITIVE

Local search is only one sliver of the search marketing game, but it is an increasingly important one, and one that is changing rapidly.

Nowadays people use the web to find local businesses, sometimes more frequently than the phone book or *Yellow Pages*. Having a presence in local search is imperative for any small business, but just as imperative is being able to compete for visibility.

There are variables to consider when mapping out your local search marketing efforts.

1. The size of the area as defined by the keyword search, or map space being viewed.
2. Google's sureness that in fact there is a business at the listed address doing what it says.
3. How Google defines the region's centre either by keyword or map parameters such as zoom level.

Traditional marketing v social marketing

It's not just about how the search engines define local results though. Businesses should also take into account how users/customers define them. Your business may be so many miles away from a user's location, but other variables can factor into this as well. Neighbourhoods may matter to users. Obstacles like rivers, for example, may matter. Maponics CEO Darrin Clement made some good points on this subject in a recent interview with *WebProNews*.

As it stands right now, there are a number of measures businesses can take to help users find them in local search. Here are four things you can do to let Google and other mapping search engines know where you're located:

☐ Have your address listed with major data providers.
☐ Claim your listing at the local business centre.
☐ Have reviews either at Google or elsewhere.
☐ List your business in the proper categories once it's been claimed.

13

DEVISING MASTER CHECKS FOR ONGOING EFFICIENCY

And so we reach the end of a journey that's only just beginning for you. But you must start where you mean to finish – at the top – and to do this effectively you need to create a series of master checks for the core aspects of your operation. Do this and you will convert every perceived problem into an opportunity; fail to do this and you open the doors to a potential early demise.

BEFORE YOU OPEN FOR BUSINESS

☐ Have I focused on a specific product or service? As a general rule, specialists outperform non-specialists. Think about this in any field: retailers, property and food (where did you buy your last takeaway pizza or chicken)? For example, if you open a fish and chip shop, it would not be a good idea to sell ice cream during summer months when the fish and chip business slows down. If you do both, you will lose the identity of being the very best in either one of them.

☐ Will further specialisation or focus improve my prospects for success? The more specialised, the better.

☐ Will my business be home-based? Online? Storefront? Franchise?

☐ Have I acknowledged my competition and limitations? It may be hard to compete with Asda or Homebase. These 'category killer' discount chains have powerful buying power and efficiencies of scale. Does your marketing plan serve a special niche?

☐ Do I understand the difference between finding a market niche and going against what the public wants? (For example, if you build a house for sale, stick with a floor plan that most buyers are seeking rather than trying to be uniquely different.)

☐ Do I have a one-year cash flow projection prepared to ensure there will be ongoing liquidity?

☐ Do I have the necessary e-commerce tools in place?

☐ Are all insurance policies in force?

☐ If I plan to sell on credit terms, is my credit rating policy in place to avoid taking on customers with poor credit ratings? (The last thing you need is to have customers who don't pay on time, and good customers will respect you for this policy.)

☐ Is my business plan complete and in written format? Does it include pre-opening, first year and long-range planning? It will play a key role in securing investors and will help uncover any weaknesses in the planning process.

☐ Have I taken the time to gain practical job experience and learn the basics of my business by first working in the business for someone else? (This is probably the best way to discover if you have made a choice that will be not only successful, but also satisfying to you.)

☐ Have I budgeted adequately for prototypes, research, sampling and trials?

☐ Have I successfully test-marketed my product or service? Was the response positive? (If not, you need to re-design, re-work, re-test – or re-think.)

☐ Have I focused on selling a great product at a fair price rather than a fair product at a great price? ('Great product' suggests a product or service with pricing power and 'fair product' suggests a commodity-type business more susceptible to competition.)

☐ Do I have all the communication, computer and other business tools in place? Do I have the skills to use them?

☐ Has my accountant fully explained the difference between hiring independent contractors and employees and the importance of compliance with Inland Revenue regulations? (While my landscaper may be an independent contractor, in most cases my sales staff will be employees and I must conform to reporting and withholding requirements.)

☐ Are the following elements of my business structure in place:
   – Is my accounting and bookkeeping system in place? Is an accountant selected?
   – Are my premises ready? This includes including having a signed lease and my tenant improvements completed.
   – Have all permits and licences been secured?
   – Has the business name been registered? Check with my solicitor.
   – Are computers, telephones, mobiles, fax and utilities operating?
   – Are graphics for advertising and promotional materials ready?
   – Is the domain name registered and the website online?
   – Is the infrastructure in place for e-business, if appropriate?
   – Are all security systems in place including protection of premises, shrinkage control and internal security?
   – Have I selected and trained the number of employees I will need?
   – Have I determined my personal work schedule?
   – Have I included my requirements for managers, consultants, independent contractors, agents and sales representatives?

EMPLOYING THE RIGHT PEOPLE

Most business owners agree on this: the toughest part of being an employer is finding and keeping good staff. Begin your search for good employees as soon as you decide that you are going to be an entrepreneur.

- ☐ Define what you need from employees.
- ☐ List the characteristics you require.
- ☐ Network: get the word out that you are looking for help.
- ☐ Develop and maintain sources for building your workforce.
- ☐ Consider family members, retired workers and students.

Alarm Bell

If you haven't already done so, give your attention to the five pointers above. Finding good staff at the outset is contingent upon the recruitment policy you devise; get this right and keeping them becomes easier.

Your customers need to feel confident that they are dealing with people who are knowledgeable and helpful. Five characteristics customers like most when dealing with a sales or service person are:

1. product or service knowledge
2. presentable appearance
3. courtesy
4. honesty
5. sincerity.

To achieve these qualities, look for marketing employees who:

- ☐ like what they do
- ☐ are quick learners who have curiosity to expand their knowledge
- ☐ project a pleasant and positive image
- ☐ like people and relate well to them
- ☐ are helpful to customers as well as to fellow associates
- ☐ are ambitious and hope someday to have your job.

Here's a checklist for hiring and training your marketing team:

- ☐ Know who you will need to hire.
- ☐ Have a hiring policy in place that includes salary structure, incentive compensation and perks.
- ☐ Create job descriptions for everyone (including for yourself), including specific skills required for each employee.
- ☐ Maintain a schedule of ongoing staff meetings to discuss product information, sales techniques and customer service.

☐ Develop policies and procedures on handling customer complaints and concerns. Keep in mind that you will get your best marketing feedback from an **unhappy** customer.

☐ Develop clear protocols for handling customers via telephone, fax or email.

☐ Continuously re-define the skills and requirements needed by new employees.

EVOLVING YOUR PURCHASING POLICY

☐ Buy only what you think you can sell.

☐ Never place an order without knowing price and terms.

☐ Purchase orders must be in writing.

☐ Have complete specifications.

☐ Buy subject to your contingencies.

☐ Have back-up sources.

☐ Be loyal to good suppliers.

☐ Have promises and extras verified in writing.

☐ Insist on price protection.

☐ Try to award the order to the lowest bidder.

☐ Don't be hesitant about repeatedly contacting suppliers to expedite needed merchandise. It's the squeaky wheels that get the grease.

☐ Communicate complaints.

☐ Use internal controls for ordering and receiving.

☐ Count and inspect everything as received.

☐ Use an inventory control system.

☐ Ask for and take term discounts.

☐ Pay on time.

☐ Pay only after verification.

☐ Watch your cash flow.

☐ Consider suppliers as a source of financing.

☐ It is better to pull suppliers your way, not push them. Be nice.

Sporadic checking of the debtors' list is a sure-fire route to disaster for small business. Allocate some time *every* day for chasing tardy debtors; that way you will always be in command of cash flow.

AVOIDING COMMON START-UP ERRORS

☐ Undue haste.

☐ Lack of focus: specialise.

☐ Lack of hands-on experience.

☐ Inadequate research and testing: test market everything first.

☐ Lack of a well thought-out business plan.

☐ Lack of working capital.

☐ Unprofessional decor, theme, logo, stationery, attire, packaging, ads and website.

☐ Not opening *quietly* to work out the shortcomings.

- ☐ Poor signage: signs should be big, clear and readable – simple is good.
- ☐ Untrained staff.
- ☐ Poor relationship with vendors.
- ☐ Unfocused marketing plan.
- ☐ Not using the advertising media that works best for your specific business.
- ☐ Skimping on insurance.
- ☐ Ignoring possible problems.
- ☐ Not recognising your limitations.

DOING THE RIGHT THINGS TO ENSURE SUCCESS

- ☐ Develop a mailing list now.
- ☐ Watch for growth possibilities and plan growth direction.
- ☐ Join your trade association and subscribe to trade magazines (stay current).
- ☐ Continue to review, develop and update your business plan, stating how you will market your product or service.
- ☐ Continue to develop your budget including proposed expenses for displays, signs, advertising, promotions and website marketing.
- ☐ Begin a file for merchandising and marketing ideas.
- ☐ Take seminars and classes.
- ☐ Read current trade magazines, papers and books, attend openings and promotions of businesses like yours.
- ☐ Develop and maintain an employee handbook.
- ☐ Talk to anyone and everyone in your field and collect business cards.
- ☐ Prepare a plan for growth possibilities.
- ☐ List potential problems and possible solutions.
- ☐ Become personally involved in selling your product or service.
- ☐ Keep your skills and knowledge current.
- ☐ Keep a journal to include your dreams of having your own business.

MOTIVATING AND REWARDING KEY PERSONNEL

By rewarding key employees through profit participation, you create the engine that will drive your managers to success. And, the greater their success (and reward), the more your overall business will benefit. Here are three types of plans (there are many) that have been used to structure a manager's incentive.

- ☐ **Leveraged plan**

  Managers receive all, or a large part of, unit earnings over a fixed target. This has been used successfully by fast food chains that are company owned and operated (rather than franchised units). Here is an example of a simplified weekly income statement of a bakery shop that is operated by a company employee-manager. This plan is 'leveraged' because every penny saved becomes a penny going into the manager's bonus cheque.

Sales		£5,000
Wages	£1,500	
Purchases	£1,500	
All other expenses (including company profit) £1,500		
Total expenses	£4,500	£4,500
Weekly profit and manager's bonus:		**£500**

□ **Unleveraged profit sharing plan**

In this case your manager receives a percentage of earnings of his or her profit centre. Here is an example:

Sales		£5,000
Wages	£1,500	
Purchases	£1,500	
All other (actual) expenses	£500	
Total expenses	£3,500	£3,500
Net profit		£1,500
Manager bonus @ 10%		**£150**

□ **Commission plan**

In this plan, the manager receives a percentage of sales for the accounting period. Assuming, as above, that sales for the period are £5,000 and the commission is 5 per cent, the compensation would be £250. In many instances, commission incentive is not appropriate because it does not include provisions for expenses. Your manager could get rich while you go broke. But commission incentive can work well when the manager does not control pricing. Salespersons in a retail clothing store would be a good example of a commission structure.

CREATING PROFIT CENTRES

□ **Create a separate profit centre for each expansion unit**. This means separate profit and loss statements for each manager.

□ **Make the accounting periods very short**. When there are not big fluctuations in inventories or other costs, even weekly profit and loss statements work well. But, if possible, don't wait for six or twelve months to reward managers. Rewards are best when received early.

☐ **Keep your profit sharing incentive plan simple and clear**. It will avoid misunderstandings and misinterpretations. Use simple words and simple accounting.

☐ **Have all your profit sharing agreements in writing**. It will avoid innocent differences of interpretation. A ball painted half black and half white is going to look differently depending on where you are viewing the ball.

☐ **Check out how your best competitor motivates their managers**. Your competitors may have already come up with a system that is most appropriate for your particular business.

THE UPS AND DOWNS OF STARTING UP

Do's

☐ Save money.
☐ Stay in a field you love.
☐ Know your business before you start (work for someone else in it).
☐ Copycat the winners in your business.
☐ Specialise, even to a single product.
☐ Find a product or service that is:
  – needed or desired
  – considered by customers to have no close substitute
  – not subject to price regulation.
☐ Set a cap on your liability.
☐ Learn computer skills.
☐ Learn communication skills.
☐ Have a lawyer, accountant, and insurance agent before you start.
☐ Prepare a business plan.
☐ Prepare the site criteria model for your particular business.
☐ Do 'for' and 'against' lists for major decisions.
☐ Buy when everyone is selling (and vice versa).
☐ Deal with those you like, trust and admire.
☐ Learn accounting.
☐ Create your own internal control plan.
☐ Keep going to school in subjects important to you.
☐ Give back to the community.

Don'ts

☐ Never sign a lease without your lawyer's review.
☐ Don't rush: there is no such thing as the last good deal.
☐ Avoid a commodity business (one without pricing power).
☐ Don't burn bridges of job security to start a business if you can help it.
☐ Don't become a business zombie: take time off.
☐ Don't compete with category killers (Asda or Toys-R-Us) unless you have a special niche.

IDENTIFYING COMMON COMMERCIAL PROBLEMS

Now let's identify some of the common mistakes made when businesses begin to grow. These mistakes can be deadly, so benefit from the others who have gone before you.

☐ **Uncontrolled cash flow**. People fail because they run out of money. When you run out of cash, you crash. So, prepare your cash flow projections for expansion very conservatively. In projections, be sure to:
– forecast income (sales) very low
– forecast expenses very high
– provide for unanticipated contingencies.

☐ **A drop in sales or insufficient sales**. If this happens, your income and cash flow will be impacted. Immediately take the necessary remedial steps by ruthlessly cutting costs.

☐ **Higher costs**. Can you increase volume of sales? Can you offset with higher prices?

☐ **New competition**. The reality of the entrepreneur's life. Can you learn from them? Can you neutralise their opening impact?

☐ **Business recessions**. You will need to promptly cut costs to maintain earnings and cash flow.

☐ **Incompetent managers or employees**. Act swiftly to rid yourself of them.

☐ **Dishonesty, theft**. Study the ways your most successful competitor controls all forms of dishonesty that your business is exposed to including shrinkage (shoplifting) and employee dishonesty. Each business will be different.

☐ **A combination of any or all of the above**.

HANDLING THREATENING SCENARIOS

☐ Identify and acknowledge your problems with brutal honesty.

☐ Immediately reduce your losses by unemotionally cutting your costs to maintain a positive cash flow and profitability. This is the **first and most important** action to take.

☐ Don't switch horses. Stay with the business you know unless its future is fatally defective.

☐ Take the initiative to explain to your creditors what your problems are: slow or smaller payments will be necessary. Never write post-dated cheques or send late payments without an explanation.

☐ Don't cut the value or quality of your products or services. Make them even better.

☐ Improve every aspect you can of your performance and image.

- ☐ Look for opportunity in adversity. Sometimes there will be bargain opportunities during business slumps.

- ☐ Remember that businesses have cycles. So, hang in there and ride out the adverse periods.

Sound rule-of-thumb activities

- ☐ Review case histories of the most successful businesses in your field.
- ☐ Review the case histories of businesses you know that failed to determine the reasons they failed. Was it inadequate testing, planning and experience?
- ☐ Identify a typical business problem in your intended business and plan a solution.
- ☐ Identify a combination of problems in your business and plan a solution.

THE TOP TEN DO'S WHEN STARTING A BUSINESS

1. Live frugally to build a start-up nest egg.
2. Be sure your intended business has long-term economic potential.
3. Aim to become a specialist.
4. Work first for someone else in your intended business.
5. Adapt to your local market and tastes.
6. Prepare a business plan before you start.
7. Learn computer and e-commerce skills before you start.
8. Have a lawyer and accountant before you start.
9. Know how to keep score: learn accounting.
10. Prepare frequent cash flow projections.

THE TOP TEN DON'TS WHEN STARTING A BUSINESS

1. Don't quit your job until you are certain you can go it alone.
2. Don't be impatient in selecting a business.
3. Don't sign a lease or franchise agreement without a lawyer.
4. Don't seek out a too highly challenging business; wait for the fat pitch.
5. Don't skimp on insurance coverage.
6. Don't be better at opening stores than operating them.
7. Don't overlook adequate employee training and motivating.
8. Don't let *anyone* sign your cheques.
9. Don't let *anyone* sign purchase orders.
10. Don't hesitate to promptly cut costs in business downturns.

If you have a question or would like to discuss any aspect of this book, feel free to contact me jimgreen@writing-for-profit.com

14

MONITORING GROWTH USING AN AUDIT CHECKLIST

Sometimes a small business fails because the owner is unaware of the many elements that can prevent the operation from growing and becoming successful, and this because the business is organised around the manager's specific area of expertise, such as marketing, accounting or production. Such specialised expertise often prevents the owner from recognising problems that may arise in other areas of the enterprise. This chapter provides the small business entrepreneur with the essentials for conducting a comprehensive search to locate existing or potential problems and for addressing opportunities as they arise.

This instrument is not exhaustive – i.e. the reader must rely on personal judgment and previous experience. However, it does provide a systematic framework to ensure that critical areas have been addressed before action is taken. **The audit is a tool, not a replacement for good management skills**. Audits cannot do your job. However, effectively designed instruments such as this audit can save valuable time for the seasoned professional as well as the novice small business manager.

HOW TO USE THE AUDIT FOR MAXIMUM EFFECTIVENESS

- ☐ **Answer all questions** with an affirmative indicating no problem or a negative indicating the presence of a problem in a specific area.
- ☐ **Review the analysis** of each section of the audit to determine what action is most appropriate.

THE AUDIT ANALYSIS

The audit analysis focuses on a variety of elements under seven critical business functions: *basic planning, general bookkeeping and accounting practices, financial planning, sales and marketing, advertising and promotion, personnel and production* – and these functions under three major audits:

- ☐ the **management** audit
- ☐ the **operations** audit
- ☐ the **financial** audit.

In the healthy and financially sound small business, these seven functional areas are in balance. However, the reader cannot work on all seven areas of the audit at once; you must decide on which areas to concentrate, based on past practices and the needs of your enterprise. Regular use of this audit instrument will help to make you more efficient in managing your business affairs.

Audit checklist for growing businesses

The management audit

- ☐ basic planning
- ☐ personnel.

The operations audit

- ☐ production
- ☐ sales and marketing
- ☐ advertising and promotion.

The financial audit

- ☐ general bookkeeping and accounting practices
- ☐ financial planning and loan proposals.

The management audit

I. Basic Planning

Yes No

A. The business has a clearly defined mission.
1. There is a written mission statement.
2. The business is carrying out the mission.
3. Mission statement is modified when necessary.
4. Employees understand and share in the mission.

B. The business has a written sales plan.
1. Market niche has been identified.
2. New product lines are developed when appropriate.
3. Targeted customers are being reached.
4. Sales are increasing.

C. The business has an annual budget.
1. Budget is used as a flexible guide.
2. Budget is used as a control device.
3. Actual expenditures are compared against budgeted expenditures.
4. Corrective action is taken when expenses are over budget.
5. Owner prepares budget.
6. The budget is realistic.

D. The business has a pricing policy.
1. Products or services are competitively priced.
2. Business provides volume discounts.
3. Prices are increased when warranted.
4. There is a relationship between pricing changes and sales volume.
5. New prices are placed on last-in goods when the price on old stock gets changed.

II. Personnel

A. Employees know what is expected of them.
1. Each employee has only one supervisor.
2. Supervisors have authority commensurate with responsibility.
3. Employees volunteer critical information to their supervisor.
4. Employees are using their skills on the job.
5. Employees feel adequately trained.

B. Each employee has a job description.
1. Employees can accurately describe what they do.
2. Employees do what is expected of them.
3. Workload is distributed equitably.
4. Employees receive feedback on performance.
5. Employees are rewarded for good performance.
6. Employees are familiar with company policies.
7. There is a concise policy manual.

C. Preventive discipline is used when appropriate.
1. Employees are informed when performance is below standard.
2. Unexcused absences are dealt with immediately.
3. Theft prevention measures are in place.

D. Regular employee meetings are conducted.
1. Employees' ideas are solicited at meetings.
2. An agenda is given to employees prior to the meeting.

The operations audit

I. Production

Yes No

A. The business has a good relationship with suppliers.
1. A well-documented plan addresses how to deal with suppliers.
2. Inventory delivery times are specified.
3. Levels of quality of materials and services are specified.
4. Payment terms are documented.
5. Contingency plans are provided.
6. Regular contact is made with suppliers.

B. The business provides for good inventory control.
1. Business has an inventory control formula to provide for optimum inventory levels.
2. Business has a policy on securing inventory in a timely fashion.

C. The business conducts incoming inventory inspections.
1. There is a written policy on incoming inspection.
2. Incoming inspection is being performed.
3. Incoming inspection levels of quality are documented.

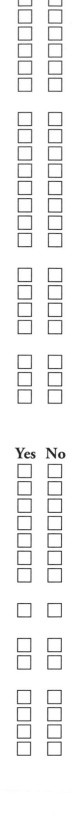

D. The business has alternate sources of raw materials. ☐ ☐
1. Two or more suppliers are identified for each product required. ☐ ☐
2. The majority of raw material requirements are divided equally between two major suppliers with a third source receiving lesser value but consistent orders. ☐ ☐

E. The business has a routine maintenance programme. ☐ ☐
1. A routine maintenance programme is documented and communicated to all maintenance personnel. ☐ ☐
2. Every major piece of equipment has a maintenance log positioned in an obvious place. ☐ ☐
3. Preventive maintenance is a regular occurrence. ☐ ☐

F. The business has a formal operator-training programme. ☐ ☐
1. Business has a written operator training manual. ☐ ☐
2. A progressive training process is in place. ☐ ☐
3. Accomplished operators are identified to answer questions from trainees. ☐ ☐
4. Constructive feedback on training progress is provided in a non-intimidating fashion. ☐ ☐

G. The business meets Health and Safety Executive (HSE) standards. ☐ ☐
1. The business is aware of HSE standards pertaining to the nature of the enterprise. ☐ ☐
2. The business conducts regular meetings with employees concerning HSE standards. ☐ ☐
3. All safety records and lost time accidents are documented. ☐ ☐

H. The business has a well-documented processing procedure. ☐ ☐
1. A scheduling process enables orders to be grouped for more efficient processing. ☐ ☐
2. A scheduling chart allowing instantaneous recognition of production status is positioned in an obvious place. ☐ ☐
3. Sub-assemblies are manufactured in sufficient quantities on a timely basis. ☐ ☐
4. Finished stock is safely transported to a clean and dry area. ☐ ☐
5. Adequate controls are provided to preclude excessive inventory build-ups that could result in finished stock spoilage or obsolescence. ☐ ☐

I. The business has an environmental awareness policy. ☐ ☐
1. A policy pertaining to the disposition of hazardous waste materials is fully documented and communicated to all relevant parties. ☐ ☐
2. Attempts are made to stay current with all existing regulations pertaining to the environment. ☐ ☐
3. Regular meetings are conducted to determine better methods of dealing with by-products. ☐ ☐

J. The business keeps up to date with technological advances. ☐ ☐
1. Company representatives attend trade shows on a regular basis. ☐ ☐
2. Business subscribes to trade publications.
3. A formal employee suggestion programme is in place. ☐ ☐
4. Business conducts regular technology advancement brainstorming sessions involving the employees. ☐ ☐
5. Business is involved in community extended learning programmes. ☐ ☐

II. Sales and Marketing

A. The owner knows exactly what the business is. ☐ ☐
1. The owner knows exactly who the customer is. ☐ ☐
2. Potential customers know about the business. ☐ ☐
3. Location is appropriate for the business. ☐ ☐
4. The market is clearly defined. ☐ ☐

B. The owner knows competitors and their location. ☐ ☐
1. The owner knows how his or her prices compare with those of the competition. ☐ ☐
2. The owner knows how the competition is regarded. ☐ ☐
3. Census data are used for strategic marketing. ☐ ☐
4. The owner is aware of regional sales patterns. ☐ ☐

C. The owner and employees focus on customer needs. ☐ ☐
1. The owner and employees treat customers courteously. ☐ ☐
2. Customer concerns, complaints and suggestions are listened to carefully. ☐ ☐
3. Customers are provided with quick, reliable service. ☐ ☐
4. Customers consider the owner knowledgeable. ☐ ☐
5. Appropriate housekeeping procedures for the business are rigidly pursued. ☐ ☐

D. The owner is aware of customer needs. ☐ ☐
1. Feedback is requested from customers. ☐ ☐
2. Sales receipts are monitored. ☐ ☐
3. Sales receipts are compared to previous years. ☐ ☐
4. Seasonal variations are taken into account. ☐ ☐

E. The business needs to increase sales volume. ☐ ☐
1. There is a sales plan in effect. ☐ ☐
2. Sales targets are being met. ☐ ☐
3. Effective sales presentations are being made to potential customers on a regular basis. ☐ ☐
4. Names of prospects are kept in a follow-up file. ☐ ☐
5. Sales are closed effectively. ☐ ☐

III. Advertising and Promotion

A. The owner has an advertising and promotional plan. ☐ ☐
1. Has an advertising budget. ☐ ☐
2. Advertises monthly. ☐ ☐
3. Advertises weekly. ☐ ☐
4. Has a promotional calendar. ☐ ☐

B. The owner uses effective advertising and promotion. ☐ ☐
1. Advertises in *Yellow Pages*. ☐ ☐
2. Uses conventional newspapers and free sheets. ☐ ☐
3. Uses radio and television advertising. ☐ ☐
4. Obtains no-cost or low-cost media coverage. ☐ ☐
5. Has its own dedicated website. ☐ ☐
6. Has a definitive online marketing strategy. ☐ ☐

C. The owner uses effective merchandising techniques. ☐ ☐
1. Relates display space to sales potential. ☐ ☐
2. Uses vendor promotional aids. ☐ ☐
3. Knows traffic flow patterns of customers. ☐ ☐
4. Ensures that all facilities are clean. ☐ ☐

D. The owner evaluates advertising and promotional efforts. ☐ ☐
1. Determines if sales increase with advertising. ☐ ☐
2. Ascertains if sales increase after special promotions. ☐ ☐
3. Ascertains whether advertising is reaching intended market. ☐ ☐

The financial audit

Yes No

I. General Bookkeeping and Accounting Practices

A. The company has a bookkeeping system. ☐ ☐
single entry ☐ double entry ☐

The owner
1. Prepares the books. ☐ ☐
a. Understands the how and why. ☐ ☐
b. Prepares own financial statements. ☐ ☐
2. Pays for bookkeeping service. ☐ ☐
a. Understands financial statements. ☐ ☐
b. Has taxes done by bookkeeper. ☐ ☐
c. Has compared cost for bookkeeper with that of a certified accountant. ☐ ☐

B. The business reconciles bank statements monthly. ☐ ☐
C. The business keeps income and expense statements accurate and prepares
statements monthly. ☐ ☐

The owner
1. Understands the purpose of financial statements. ☐ ☐
2. Compares several monthly statements for trends. ☐ ☐
3. Compares statements against industry averages. ☐ ☐
4. Knows current financial status of business. ☐ ☐

D. The business makes provision for VAT. ☐ ☐

The owner
1. Understands the procedures. ☐ ☐
2. Makes payment on time to avoid penalties. ☐ ☐
3. Provides all relevant information. ☐ ☐

E. The business has a credit policy. ☐ ☐
1. Ages billing system monthly. ☐ ☐
2. Accesses late payment fee from customers. ☐ ☐
3. Writes off bad debts. ☐ ☐
4. Has good collection policies. ☐ ☐
5. Has a series of increasingly pointed letters to collect from late customers. ☐ ☐
6. Has VISA, MasterCard, or other credit card system. ☐ ☐
7. Offers discounts for early payment. ☐ ☐

F. The company files all tax returns in a timely manner. ☐ ☐

The owner
1. Considers tax implications of equipment early. ☐ ☐
2. Considers buy versus lease possibilities. ☐ ☐

II. Financial Planning and Loan Proposals
A. The business has an adequate cash flow. ☐ ☐
1. Cash receipts are monitored and accounted for. ☐ ☐
2. Cheques are deposited properly each day. ☐ ☐
3. Customer invoicing is done promptly (within two working days). ☐ ☐
4. Collections are received within 30 days. ☐ ☐
5. Accounts payable takes advantage of cash discounts. ☐ ☐
6. Disbursements are made to best effect. ☐ ☐

B. The business projects cash-flow needs. ☐ ☐
1. Payrolls are met without problems. ☐ ☐
2. Money is set aside for expansion, emergencies and opportune purchases. ☐ ☐
3. Short-term financing is used when needed. ☐ ☐
4. Line of credit is established with a bank. ☐ ☐

C. The business understands the role of financial planning in today's highly competitive lending markets. ☐ ☐
1. The owner's personal resume is up to date. ☐ ☐
2. Personal financial statements have been prepared. ☐ ☐

3. The business has a written business plan.   ☐ ☐
4. Source and use of funds statements exist for the past two years, with a
    projection for the next two years.   ☐ ☐
5. An accurate balance sheet exists for the past two years and includes a
    projection for the next two years.   ☐ ☐
6. The owner has a good working relationship with the bank.   ☐ ☐
7. There is a strong debt-to-equity ratio.   ☐ ☐

Complete an initial audit and you will readily appreciate why the seven critical business functions – *basic planning, general bookkeeping and accounting practices, financial planning and loan proposals, sales and marketing, advertising and promotion, personnel and production* – dovetail and interrelate – and why it is vital for the growth of your enterprise that you undertake these audits on a regular basis. While this particular model for an audit checklist has a strong manufacturing bias, you may alter, edit or completely restructure the format to meet with your own specific requirements.

GLOSSARY OF BUSINESS TERMS

Ability to repay. Evidence of the wherewithal to repay any loans you arrange in connection with your enterprise.

Accommodation facility. Arrangement with (say) your Local Development Business Centre for short-term rental of desk space, secretarial services, mail handling, etc.

Annual accounts. Formal statements showing the financial position of a business, which are normally drawn up by an accountant and submitted to the Inland Revenue for tax assessment purposes. They usually comprise a trading account, a profit and loss account and a balance sheet.

Assets. The total value of things owned by a business.

Attachments. Computer files that accompany the message portion of an email.

Autoresponder. An electronic internet email device which collects enquiries and which has the capability of transmitting up to seven individual responses – from immediate to follow ups.

Bizops. Universally accepted internet jargon for business opportunities.

Book-keeping. The production of records of a business's financial transactions.

Booster grant. Local Authority Start-Up Grant (typically around £1,000).

Business administration refresher course. Local Authority crash course on business skills (normally free of charge to qualified applicants).

Business Development Executive. Your initial contact on matters relating to starting up.

Business plan. The masterplan you prepare to convince other people that you have what it takes to run a business.

Buying signals. The telltale signs that indicate you're talking to a willing buyer.

Cash book. The accounting book which records all payments into and out of the business's bank account.

Cash flow. Controlling the flow of cash you collect from customers and other sources before you pay your suppliers and any other creditors.

Collateral. Security put up against loan arrangements, for example a house or insurance policy.

Competitive activity. Activity by your competitors in such matters as pricing, promotions, sales territory, marketing.

Contact points. Your essential personal points of contact when conducting sales negotiation. They are not always the decision makers, though.

Conversion ratios. The relationship between the number of calls you have to make to achieve a given number of confirmed sales, for example 36 calls, 12 sales. Divide 12 into 36 and the conversion ratio is 3.

Creditors. The suppliers to the business to whom money is owed and the amount owed by the business to them (contrast debtors).

Current assets. These are assets which are either cash or can be turned into cash quite quickly. They include cash, bank balances (not overdrafts), debtors, stock and work in progress. (Contrast current liabilities and fixed assets.)

Current liabilities. These are amounts owed to suppliers (creditors) together with short-term loans such as bank overdrafts. Short-term loans are those less than one year and so part of hire purchase liabilities may also be included under this heading where they are repayable within the next twelve months. (Contrast current assets.)

Customer base. The total number of customers with whom you are currently doing business.

Customer service. The added extras which businesses provide to ensure continued customer satisfaction, thus achieving loyalty amongst the purchasers of products and services.

Debtors. The customers of the business who owe money to the business and the amount owed. (Contrast creditors.)

Depreciation. An allowance made (charged as an expense in the profit and loss account) for the reduction in value of fixed assets (particularly machinery, furnishings and motor vehicles) during each accounting period.

Direct mail. Advertising and promotional material delivered to a specific and carefully targeted audience.

Discretionary funds. That amount of money you have available for paying out as you please.

Distribution channels. The patterns of distribution you have determined for your product, for example, wholesale, retail, door-to-door, direct mail.

Downlines. Those participants operating in downward levels from the sponsor in multi level marketing.

Email. Electronic information addressed and transmitted over the internet.

Email address. Consists of a user ID, followed by an @ sign and a domain name. For example:
jimgreen@writing-for-profit.com

Entrepreneur. A business person who seeks to make a profit by risk and initiative.

Entrepreneurship training programme. Courses largely underwritten by government agencies, conducted by entrepreneurs in their own right and dealing exclusively with essential entreprencurial skills.

Equity stake. Capital invested in an enterprise on a long-term or permanent basis. All or part of the share capital.

Executive summary. The concise précis of what your enterprise is all about and which appears at the very beginning of your business plan.

External capital. The amount of money (loans, grants, overdraft) you need to raise from outside sources.

Fixed assets. Items of long-term use to a business such as a freehold property, fixtures and fittings.

Fixed interest rates. Those rates which are set when funding is arranged and do not vary for a given period.

Flame. An internet message which uses profanity or otherwise belittles the recipient.

Founders' equity. The respective amounts of money each of the founding members invest in an enterprise.

Franchise. A licence for one party to set up and run a venture in a particular area for a specific period of time, using the trading name and business format of another party.

Franchisee. The party buying a franchise. (The party granting the franchise is known as a franchisor.)

Full repairing and insuring liability. A legal obligation whereby the tenant of a property is responsible for its internal and external maintenance and insurance.

Funds sourcing. Going out in the market looking for the external capital you need to get the business up and running.

Free initial training. Available in various categories (free of charge to recognised start-ups) from public sector sources.

Going concern. A well established business which appears to be trading satisfactorily (although an examination of its books and accounts may convey a different and more accurate image).

Goodwill. Sum based on the annual net profit of a business and added to its value when sold.

Gross profit. The profit derived from buying and selling goods and services, before the deduction of overheads such as rent, wages and transport costs.

Hands-on experience. Practical knowledge gained through participation as opposed to academic study.

Hidden agenda. An important and real agenda which isn't written down on any official piece of paper.

Image. The impression you give to others of yourself and your business.

Immediate catchment area. The geographical area in which you initially intend to do business.

Indigenous growth. Creating growth in the economy through encouraging locally based enterprise.

Information technology. Using computers to store and process information as opposed to entrusting it all to pen and paper.

Initial budgeting requirements. Estimating precisely how much money you will need by way of investment and sales to keep you afloat during the initial trading period.

Input tax. Value added tax charged on products and services purchased by a VAT registered trader for resale or business use.

Intelligence gathering. The continuous gathering of information about your industry so that you always know what's happening.

Internet. A worldwide network of millions of computers and servers that uses telephone system technology to transmit information from one place to another.

Internet Service Provider (ISP). A company which provides users access to the internet.

Jointly and severally responsible. Expression used in relation to partnerships, indicating that partners are responsible for each others' activities.

Liabilities. The money which a business owes in the forms of loans, hire purchase agreements, trade suppliers, tax, etc.

Limited company. A separate legal entity which can trade in its own right. Forming limited companies can have tax advantages, and can protect the owners from paying debts if the firm runs into trouble.

Mainstream finance. Just another way of describing external finance: mainstream because it normally accounts for the bulk of the required investment.

Marketplace. Where you'll be doing business.

Marketing grants. Available only from the public sector and only to qualified start-ups for assistance with brochures, exhibition participation, etc.

Marketing programme. The programme of activity that gets your business rolling.

Modem. A device that allows your computer to talk to other computers using your telephone line. Modems range in speeds of 9.6 to 33.6 Kb per second.

MLM (multi level marketing). Marketing of a product or service at various levels in upward and downward directions.

Net assets. The total of **net current assets** added to **fixed assets**.

Net current assets. The sum remaining after **current liabilities** have been deducted from **current assets**.

Net profit. The profit of a business after taking account of all expenses.

Networking. Broadcasting your message to groups of people and achieving a knock-on effect in the performance of your sales programme.

Output tax. Value added tax charged by a VAT registered trader on goods and services sold to customers.

Overheads. Costs incurred by a business regardless of its sales turnover.

Participating equity partner. A partner in the enterprise who has contributed to the share capital.

Partnership. A legally binding business association of two or more people. Each partner is usually equally liable for all of the partnership's debts.

Pay As You Earn (PAYE). A scheme whereby employers have to deduct tax and national insurance from employees' wages to pass them to the Inland Revenue each month.

Personal drawings. Monies taken out of a business for personal use, as noted on the balance sheet.

Personal integrity. Your personal honesty and trustworthiness. It is your most vital asset in business.

Pricing policy. The means you use to set your selling prices.

Profit and loss account. An account summarising the income and expenditure of a business for a given period and showing the surplus income (profit) or deficit (loss).

Planning permission. The legal permission which is granted by local authorities for individuals or businesses to build or change the use of premises. Planning permission may be necessary for some home-based businesses.

Professional indemnity. An insurance scheme which protects businesses against claims for problems involved in the running of the business, such as administrative errors.

Proven ideas. Business ideas that are tried, tested and seen to work in practice.

Public sector funding. Working capital obtained from the public sector by way of grants and soft loans.

Sale or return. A trading condition whereby unsold stock is returned to the supplier for a cash refund or credit against future purchases.

Scenario planning. Planning for various 'what if' situations that could occur in the future.

Schematic. A simple diagram that illustrates an idea.

Secured borrowings. Loans, overdrafts, mortgages and other financial advantages against which assets have been set by a borrower.

Security. Assets pledged by a borrower against monies borrowed, to protect the lender against defaults by the borrower.

Seed capital. The initial cash invested in a business to get it up and running.

Selling off-the-page. Getting distribution of a product or service solely by means of press advertising.

Server. Any computer or device on a network that manages network resources.

Skills Funding Agency. This public sector agency is part of a network of organisations that commission, manage and market training for adults.

Soft loans. So called because they are arranged on very generous terms. They are available only from the public sector.

Sole trader. A self-employed individual.

Start-up. A brand new enterprise.

Stock. Finished items which are ready to be sold to customers.

Telemarketing techniques. Using the telephone (and fax) to sell direct to customers.

Template. A pattern for success, your business plan.

Trade directories. Every trade has at least one reference directory, classifying businesses according to their trading profiles.

Trading name. The name under which your enterprise will trade.

Trading out of your debts. Trying to pay off old debts by creating new business. It is normally a road to ruin.

Turnover. The total amount of money which comes into a business from all sources.

Uniform Resource Locator (URL). The standard address used to locate a web page, web server, or other device on the web or on the internet.

Unsecured loans. Loans made without any collateral.

VAT. Value Added Tax. A tax applied to a wide range of products and services, currently 17.5 per cent.

VAT threshold. The trading level at which you are obliged to register for Value Added Tax. It is currently £68,000 pa, but may be changed each year in the Chancellor's Budget.

Venture capital houses. Financial institutions you would go to first for funding if your enterprise is on a major scale.

Website. A collection of world wide web documents, normally consisting of a home page and several related pages i.e. an interactive electronic book.

Working capital. The amount of money required to keep the business running effectively and solvently.

World wide web (WWW). The graphical segment of the internet, which consists of millions of web pages on servers all over the world. Each page carries an address called an URL and contains links which you click to go to other web pages.

Young People's Learning Agency. Government sponsored projects to help young unemployed persons find a job or set up in business for themselves.

Appendix 1:
SOURCES OF PUBLIC SECTOR ASSISTANCE

SKILLS FUNDING AGENCY

The Skills Funding Agency is an agency of the Department for Business, Innovation and Skills (BIS). Its job is to fund and regulate adult FE and skills training in England.

The Agency is part of a network of organisations in the country that commission, manage and market training for adults.

Its mission is to ensure that people and businesses can access the skills training they need to succeed in playing their part in society and in growing England's economy. They do this in the context of policy set by BIS and informed by the needs of businesses, communities and regions, and sector and industry bodies.

The Skills Funding Agency employs around 1,200 staff at their head office in Coventry and in 21 offices around England (http://skillsfundingagency.bis.gov.uk).

YOUNG PEOPLE'S LEARNING AGENCY

Responsibility for The Young People's Learning Agency (YPLA) lies with the Department for Education. It supports the delivery of education and training to young people in England. The YPLA champions young people by:

- ☐ providing financial support to young learners;
- ☐ funding academies for all their provision;
- ☐ supporting local authorities in fulfilling their new duties for commissioning education and training for all 16–19 year old learners in England.

The YPLA also funds and manages the performance of academies and provides direct support for learners, in particular the Education Maintenance Allowance, for people aged between 16 and 19.

There are currently 203 academies open in 83 local authority areas in England, with up to 100 others due to open by September 2010 (http://www.ypla.gov.uk).

SCOTTISH ENTERPRISE

Business advice and support for Scotland's growing businesses (http://www.scottish-enterprise.com).

Appendix 2
THE INTERNET

Internet training
Mike Filsaime *http://www.mikefilsaime.com*
Ewan Chia *http://www.ewenchia.com*
Derek Gyle *http://www.marketingchallenge.com*
Marlon Sanders *http://www.marlonsnews.com*
Michael Green *http://howtocorp.com*

Web hosts for small business
SiteSell *http://sitesell.com*
ThirdSphere *http://thirdsphere.com*

Electronic publishing
Adobe *http://adobe.com*
PDF 995 *http://PDF995.com*

Automatic article submitters
Automatic Article Submitter *http://www.automaticarticlesubmitter.com*
Article Submitter PRO *http://articlesubmitterpro.com*

Autoresponders for small business
A Weber *http://aweber.com*
Get Response *http://getresponse.com*

File Transfer Protocol (FTP)
Ipswitch *http://ipswitch.com*

Online Payment Processors
ClickBank *http://clickbank.com*
PayPal *http://paypal.com*

Online communications
Skype *http://skype.com*

Online security
Norton *http://norton.com*

Web graphics software
http://www.webgraphicsoft.com

Web cameras
Logitech *http://logitech.com*
Earth Cam *http://www.earthcam.com*

Social media

Facebook *http://facebook.com*
My Space *http://myspace.com*
Squidoo *http://squidoo.com*
Hub Pages *http://hubpages.com*
YouTube *http://youtube.com*
Bebo *http://bebo.com*
Dailymotion *http://dailymotion.com*
hi5 *http://hi5.com*
Gather *http://gather.com*

Social bookmarking

Propellor *http://propeller.com*
Slashdot *http://slashdot.org*
Digg *http://digg.com*
Technorati *http://technorati.com*
Delicious *http://delicious*
StumbleUpon *http://stumbleupon.com*
Twitter *http://twitter.com*
Reddit *http://reddit.com*
Fark *http://fark.com*
Newsvine *http://newsvine.com*
SWiK *http://swik.net*
Connotea *http://connotea.org*
Sphinn *http://sphinn.com*
BlinkList *http://blinklist.com*
Faves *http://faves.com*
Mister Wong *http://mister-wong.com*
Spurl.net *http://spurl.net*
Netvouz *http://netvouz.com*
Diigo *http://diigo.com*
RawSugar *http://rawsugar.com*
BibSonomy *http://bibsonomy.org*
folkd.com *http://folkd.com*
linkaGoGo *http://linkagogo.com*

Useful reading

How to Grow Your Small Business Rapidly Online How To Books ISBN 9781845281595

Government

Doing Business Online
http://www.businesslink.gov.uk/bdotg/action/layer?r.s=tl&r.lc=en&topicId=1073861197

BUSINESS ADDRESS BOOK

A short book of this kind can only be a guide to the way to set up a business of your own. You will no doubt need further information and advice on starting your business, running it, and expanding in the future. To help you find that information and advice, here is a comprehensive list of contacts which may be of help.

STARTING UP

Business in the Community, 8 Stratton Street, London W1X 6AH. Tel: (020) 7629 1600.

Companies Registration Office, 55 City Road, London EC1Y 1BB. Tel: (020) 7253 9393. Also at: Companies House, Crown Way, Cardiff CF4 3UZ. Tel: (01222) 388588.

Council for Small Industries in Rural Areas, 141 Castle Street, Salisbury, Wiltshire SP1 3TP. Tel: (01722) 336255.

Department of Trade and Industry (DTI), 1–19 Victoria Street, London SW1Y 0ET. Tel: (020) 7215 7877.

DTI Loan Guarantee Section, Level 2, St Mary's House, c/o Moorfoot, Sheffield S1 4PQ. Tel: (0114) 2597308/9.

National Business Names Registry, Somerset House, Temple Street, Birmingham B5 2DP. Tel: (0121) 643 0227.

Prince's Youth Business Trust, 5 Cleveland Place, London SW1Y 6JJ. Tel: (020) 7925 2900.

Small Firms Information Service, Abell House, John Islip Street, London SW1P 4LN. Dial 100 and ask for FREEPHONE ENTERPRISE.

Registrar of Business Names, London Chamber of Commerce, 33 Queen Street, London EC4R 1BX. Tel: (020) 7248 4444.

Registrar of Companies, 21 Bothwell Street, Glasgow G2 6NL. Tel: (0141) 248 3315.

Wyvern Business Library, 6 The Business Park, Ely, Cambridgeshire CB7 4JW. Tel: (01352) 665544. Supplies a range of practical business and self improvement books by direct mail.

MEMBERSHIP ORGANISATIONS

Alliance of Small Firms and Self-Employed People Ltd, 33 The Greene, Calne, Wiltshire SN11 8DJ. Tel: (01249) 817003.

The Association of British Chambers of Commerce, 9 Tufton Street, London SW1P 3QB. Tel: (020) 7222 1555.

Business Link. Tel: 0800 104010. Business support services.

Federation of Small Businesses, 32 Orchard Road, Lytham St Annes FY8 1NY. Tel: (01253) 720911.

Association of Independent Businesses, 26 Addison Place, London W11 4RJ. Tel: (020) 7371 1299.

British Franchise Association, Thames View, Newton Road, Henley on Thames, Oxfordshire

RG9 1HG. Tel: (01491) 578049.

Confederation of British Industry, Centre Point, 103 Oxford Street, London WC1A 1DU. Tel: (020) 7379 7400.

Federation of Small Businesses, 140 Lower Marsh, Westminster Bridge, London SE1 7AE. Tel: (020) 7928 9272.

Institute of Directors, 116 Pall Mall, London SW1Y 5EA. Tel: (020) 7839 1233.

National Federation of Self Employed and Small Businesses, 32 St Annes Road West, Lytham St Annes, Lancashire FY8 1NY. Tel: (01253) 720911. And at:

Unit 101c Argent Centre, 60 Frederick Street, Birmingham B1 3HB. Tel: (0121) 236 6849.

11 Great George Street, Bristol, Avon BS1 5QY. Tel: (0117) 9276073.

34 Argyle Street, Glasgow G2 8BD. Tel: (0141) 221 0775.

35a Appletongate, Newark, Nottinghamshire NG24 1JR. Tel: (01636) 7101311.

National Market Traders' Federation, Hampton House, Hawshaw Lane, Hoyland, Barnsley, S74 0HA. Tel: (01226) 749021.

OwnBase, 68 First Avenue, Bush Hill Park, Enfield EN1 1BN. An organisation established to help people working from home.

RAISING FINANCE

Abbey National plc, Abbey House, Baker Street, London NW1 6XL. Tel: (020) 7486 5555.

American Express, PO Box 63, Brighton, Sussex BN1 1YZ. Tel: (01273) 696933.

Bank of Scotland, The Mound, Edinburgh EH1 1YZ. Tel: (0131) 243 5441.

Banking Information Service, 10 Lombard Street, London EC3V 9AT. Tel: (020) 7626 8486.

Barclays Banks PLC, 54 Lombard Street, London EC3N 3HJ. Tel: (020) 7626 1567.

Chartered Association of Certified Accountants, 29 Lincoln's Inn Fields, London WC2. Tel: (020) 7242 6855.

Clydesdale Bank PLC, 150 Buchanan Street, Glasgow G1. Tel: (0141) 248 7070.

Co-operative Bank PLC, PO Box 101, 1 Balloon Street, Manchester M60 4EP. Tel: (0161) 832 3456.

Finance and Leasing Association, 18 Upper Grosvenor Street, London W1X 9PB. Tel: (020) 7491 2783.

Institute of Chartered Accountants in England and Wales, PO Box 433, Chartered Accountants Hall, Moorgate Place, London EC2P 2BJ. Tel: (020) 7920 8100.

Institute of Chartered Accountants of Scotland, 27 Queen Street, Edinburgh EH2 1LA. Tel: (0131) 225 5673.

Institute of Management Consultants, 32 Hatton Garden, London EC1N 8DL. Tel: (020) 7242 2140.

Lloyds Bank PLC, PO Box 215, 71 Lombard Street, London EC3P 3BS. Tel: (020) 7626 1500.

Midland Bank PLC, 27 Poultry, London EC2P 2BX. Tel: (020) 7260 8000. Now a subsidiary of the Hong Kong & Shanghai Bank.

National Westminster Bank PLC, 41 Lothbury, London EC2P 2BP. Tel: (020) 7726 1000. It also owns Coutts & Co.

Nationwide Anglia Building Society, Chesterfield Road, Bloomsbury Way, London WC1V 6PW. Tel: (020) 7242 8822.

Office of the Banking Ombudsman, Citadel House, 5/11 Fetter Lane, London EC4A 1BR. Tel: (020) 7404 9944.

Royal Bank of Scotland, PO Box 31, 42 St Andrew Square, Edinburgh EH2 2YE. Tel: (0131) 556 8555.

3i PLC, 91 Waterloo Road, London SE1 8XP. Tel: (020) 7928 3131.

TSB Group PLC, 25 Milk Street, London EC2V 8LU. Tel: (020) 7606 7070.

MARKETING

Advertising Standards Authority, Brook House, Torrington Place, London WC1. Tel: (020) 7580 5555.

Advertising Association, Abford House, 15 Wilton Road, London SW1V 1NJ. Tel: (020) 7828 2771.

Association of Illustrators, 29 Bedford Square, London W1B 3EG. Tel: (020) 7636 4100.

British Media Publications, Windsor Court, East Grinstead House, East Grinstead, West Sussex RH19 1XE. Tel: (01342) 326972.

British Promotional Merchandise Association, 21–25 Lower Stone Street, Maidstone, Kent ME15 6YT. Tel: (01622) 671081.

Chartered Institute of Marketing, Moor Hall, Cookham, Berkshire SL6 9QH. Tel: (016285) 24922.

Communications, Advertising and Marketing Education Foundation, 15 Wilton Road, London SW1V 1NJ. Tel: (020) 7828 7506. For information about training.

Direct Mail Services Standards Board, 26 Eccleston Street, London SW1W 9PY. Tel: (020) 7824 8651.

Direct Marketing Association, Haymarket House, 1 Oxendon St, London SW1Y 4EE. Tel: (020) 7321 2525.

Direct Selling Association, 29 Floral Street, London WC2E 9DP. Tel: (020) 7497 1234.

Dun and Bradstreet, Holmers Farm Way, High Wycombe HP12 4UL. Tel: (01494) 422000. A leading provider of marketing and business information about individual companies.

Institute of Practitioners in Advertising, 44 Belgrave Square, London SW1X 8QS. Tel: (020) 7235 7020.

Institute of Public Relations, 15 Northburgh Street, London EC1V 0PR. Tel: (020) 7253 5151.

Institute of Sales Promotion, 66 Pentonville Road, London N1 9HS. Tel: (020) 7837 5340.

Market Research Society, 15 Northburgh Street, London EC1V 0AH. Tel: (020) 7490 4911.

Network Marketing Association, 5 Cornwall Crescent, London W11 1PH. Tel: (020) 221 5611.

Public Relations Consultants Association, Willow House, Willow Place, London SW1P 1JH. Tel: (020) 7233 6026.

LEGAL MATTERS

British Standards Institution, 2 Park Street, London W1A 2BS. Tel: (020) 7629 9000.

Data Protection Registrar, Springfield House, Water Lane, Wilmslow, Cheshire SK9 5AX.

Tel: (01625) 535777.

Health and Safety Executive, St Hugh's House, Trinity Road, Bootle, Merseyside L20 2QY. Tel: (0151) 951 4381.

Rose Court, 2 Southwark Bridge, London SE1 9HS. Tel: (020) 7717 6000.

Broad Lane, Sheffield, Yorkshire S3 7HQ. Tel: (0114) 2892345.

Law Society (England and Wales), 113 Chancery Lane, London WC2A 1PL. Tel: (020) 7242 1222. The professional body for solicitors.

Law Society of Northern Ireland, 90–106 Victoria Street, Belfast BT1 2BJ. Tel: (028) 9023 1614.

Law Society of Scotland, 25 Drumsheugh Gardens, Edinburgh EH3 7YR. Tel: (0131) 226 7411.

Lawyers for Enterprise. Tel: (020) 7405 9075. These are solicitors who will offer a short, free initial interview concerning the general points you should consider when setting up or running a business.

Legal Aid Board, 8 Great New Street, London EC4A 3BN. Tel: (020) 7353 3794.

Office of Fair Trading, Field House, Breams Buildings, London EC4A 1HA. Tel: (020) 7242 2858.

Patent Office, 25 Southampton Buildings, Chancery Lane, London WC2A 1AY. Tel: (020) 7438 4700.

Royal Town Planning Institute, 26 Portland Place, London W1N 4BE. Tel: (020) 7636 9107.

The Trademarks Registry, 25 Southampton Buildings, Chancery Lane, London WC2A 1AY. Tel: (020) 7438 4700.

KEEPING RECORDS

Contributions Agency. The government agency responsible for collecting National Insurance payments from employers and the self-employed. See your local phone book for telephone number and address.

Customs and Excise, New King's Beam House, 22 Upper Ground, London SE1 9PJ. Tel: (020) 7620 1313. Or see your local phone book. The organisation responsible for collecting and refunding VAT payments.

Department of Social Security, Alexander Fleming House, Elephant and Castle, London SE1 6BY. Tel: (020) 7972 2000. Or see your local phone book.

DSS Leaflet Unit, PO Box 21, Stanmore, Middlesex HA7 1AY. Tel: 0800 393 539.

Inland Revenue, Somerset House, Strand, London WC2R 1LB. Tel: (020) 7438 6622. Or see your local phone book. The organisation responsible for assessing income tax, corporation tax, advance corporation tax, capital gains tax, inheritance and other taxes. Collection is undertaken by a separate organisation, The Collector of Taxes based in Yorkshire.

Please bear in mind that organisations can, and frequently do, relocate and change their phone numbers. You may need to refer to the last local telephone directory or directory enquiries.

MORE BUSINESS BOOKS TO HELP YOU

STARTING A BUSINESS
The Successful Consultant, Susan Nash (How To Books, 2nd edition 2005).
Be Your Own Boss, British Telecom Guide.
The Business of Freelancing, Graham Jones (BFP Jones 1987).
Raising Start-up Finance, Phil Stone (How To Books, 2001).
The Wyvern Business Library, Wyvern House, 7 The Business Park, Ely, Cambridgeshire CB7 4JW. Suppliers of a wide range of business books, available through mail order.
Getting Started, R Rhodes (Kogan Page, 1995).
How to be an Entrepreneur, I Phillipson (Kogan Page, 1993).
The First 12 Months, D Bangs (Kogan Page, 1993).
Working for Yourself, G Golzen (Kogan Page, 1995).
A *Guide to Working from Home*, British Telecom Guide.
Running Your Own Business – Planning for Success (Department of Employment).
Small Business Digest, quarterly (National Westminster Bank).
Small Business Insurance Advice File (Association of British Insurers).
Sources of Free Business Information, Michael Brooks (Kogan Page, 1986).
Start Up and go with NatWest (National Westminster Bank).
Starting Up Your Own Business, 3i (Investors in Industry).
Starting Your Business (Lloyds Bank).
Starting Your Own Business (Barclays Bank).
Starting a Small Business, Alan and Deborah Fowler (Warner Books).
Starting Up, G Jones (Pitman Publishing, 1991).
Swim With the Sharks, Harvey Mackay (Warner Books).
101 Great Money Making Ideas, Mark Hempshell (Northcote House).
Franchising: A Practical Guide for Franchisors and Franchisees, I Maitland (Mercury, 1991).
Setting Up a Limited Company, Robert Browning (How To Books, 4th edition, 2003).
Setting Up and Running Your Own Business, Phil Stone (How To Books, 2nd edition 2004).

ORGANISING YOURSELF
Conquering the Paper Pile-Up, Stephanie Culp (Writer's Digest Books, Cincinnati, 1990).
Getting Things Done: The ABC of Time Management, Edwin C Biss (Warner Publications).
Running Your Office, Margaret Korving (BBC, 1989).
The Seven Keys to Superefficiency, Winston Fletcher (Sidgwick & Jackson, 1986).
10-Minute Time and Stress Management, Dr David Lewis (Piatkus).
Managing Growth, M Bennett (Pitman Publishing, 1991).
Small Business Survival, R Bennett (Pitman Publishing, 1991).

BUSINESS PLANNING

The Business Planner: A Complete Guide to Raising Finance, I Maitland (Butterworth Heinemann, 1992).

The Business Plan Workbook, Colin and Paul Barrow (Kogan Page Ltd, 1988).

Business Planning & Development, a Practical Guide, Bill Elsom (First Class Publishing, Doncaster).

Preparing a Winning Business Plan, Matthew Record (How To Books, 4th edition, 2003).

How To Prepare a Business Plan (2nd edition), Edward Blackwell (Kogan Page Publishers, 1993).

The Perfect Business Plan, Ron Johnson (Century Business, 1993).

KEEPING FINANCIAL CONTROL

The Barclays Guide to Financial Management for the Small Business Peter Wilson (Blackwell Publishers, 1990).

Business Cash Books Made Easy, M Pullen (Kogan Page, 1992).

Budgeting for the Non-Financial Manager, I Maitland (Pitman Publishing, 1995).

Financial Control, D Irwin (Pitman Publishing, 1991).

Budgetary Control in the Small Company, 3i (Investors in Industry).

Book-keeping & Accounting for the Small Business, Peter Taylor (How To Books, 7th edition, 2003).

Cash Flows & Budgeting Made Easy, Peter Taylor (How To Books, 4th edition, 2002).

Cashflow & How to Improve It, Leon Hopkins (Kogan Page, 1993).

Mastering Book-Keeping, Peter Marshall (How To Books, 6th edition, 2003).

BUSINESS COMPUTING

I Hate Buying a Computer, Jim Felici (Que).

Buy a PC, Mike James (I/O Press).

Beginners Guide to the PC, McKellan and Waixel (Kuma Books).

Ten Minute Guide to the Internet & World Wide Web, Galen Grimes (QUE).

Teach Yourself the Internet in 24 Hours, Noel Estabrook (SamsNet).

Surfing Your Career, Hilary Nickell (How To Books, 2nd edition, 2001).

MARKETING & PROMOTION

Effective Negotiating, C Robinson (Kogan Page, 1995).

Don't Get Mad, Write, Bruce West (Kogan Page).

High Income Consulting, Tom Lambert (Nicholas Brealey).

How To Increase Sales by Telephone, Alfred Tack (The Windmill Press, Surrey, 1971).

How to Promote Your Own Business, Jim Dudley.

Writing a Report, John Bowden (How To Books, 7th edition, 2004).

The Language of Success, BT Booklet.

101 Ways to Get More Business, Timothy R V Foster (Kogan Page).

The Secrets of Effective Direct Mail, John Fraser-Robinson (McGraw-Hill, London 1989).

The Secrets of Successful Copywriting, Patrick Quinn (Heinemann, London).

The Secrets of Successful Low-Budget Advertising, Patrick Quinn (Heinemann, London 1987).
Seductive Selling, Kit Sadgrove (Kogan Press).
Total Confidence, Philipa Davies (Piatkus).
Write Right, A Desk Draw Digest of Punctuation, Grammar and Style, Jan Vernolia (David & Charles, London 1982).
Writing to Sell, The Complete Guide to Copywriting for Business, Kit Sadgrove (Robert Hale, London 1991).
Writing to Win, Mel Lewis (McGraw-Hill, London 1987).
The Power of Persuasion (Wyvern Business Library, 1992).
Prospecting for Customers (Wyvern Business Library, 1994).
How to Plan Direct Mail, I Maitland (Cassell, 1995).
How to Plan Press Advertising, I Maitland (Cassell, 1995).
How to Plan Radio Advertising, I Maitland (Cassell, 1995).
How to Sell a Service, Malcolm McDonald and John Leppart (Heinemann, 1986).
How to Win Customers, Heinz Goldman (Pan, London 1980).
Successful Marketing for the Small Business, Dave Patten (Kogan Page).
Successful Negotiation, R Maddux (Kogan Page, 1988).
Selling, P Allen (Pitman Publishing, 1991).

TAKING ON STAFF
Getting a Result, I Maitland (Institute of Personnel and Development, 1994).
How to Recruit, I Maitland, (Gower, 1992).
Managing Staff, I Maitland (Cassell, 1995).
Motivating People, I Maitland (Institute of Personnel and Development, 1995).
Recruiting for the Future, I Maitland (Cassell, 1995).
Modern Employment Law, M Whinchup (Butterworth Heinemann, 1995).

USING PROFESSIONAL ADVISERS
Getting Value from Professional Advisers, C Standish (Kogan Page, 1993).
Why You Need a Chartered Accountant (Institute of Chartered Accountants).

UNDERSTANDING BUSINESS LAW
Computers and the Law, David Bainbridge (Pitman, 1990).
Law for the Small Business, Patricia Clayton (Kogan Page, 1991).
A Step by Step Guide to Planning Permission for Small Businesses available from your local authority planning department.
Your Business and the Law, John Harries (Oyez Longman).
Health and Safety, V Broadhurst (Pitman Publishing, 1991).
Heath and Safety Law, J Stranks (Pitman Publishing, 1994).
Law for Small Businesses, A Holmes, R Evans, C Wright, S Wright (Pitman Publishing, 1991).

PAYING TAX
How to Cut Your Tax Bills, G Thornton (Kogan Page, 1995).

Tax for the Self-employed (Allied-Dunbar Money Guide), David Williams (Longman, 1990).

Taxman Tactics, How to play by the rules – and win, Stephen Courtney (Sidgwick and Jackson, 1990).

Taxation, T Docherty (Pitman Publishing, 1994).

Taxes on Business, K Armstrong (Kogan Page, 1994).

Understanding VAT, W Lovell (Pitman Publishing, 1991).

The VAT Guide (HM Customs and Excise).

BUSINESS PERIODICALS

Home Run, 'The action guide to working successfully for yourself.' Active Information, 79 Black Lion Lane, London W6 9BG. Tel: (0181) 846 9244.

OwnBase: The Newsletter for Home-based Workers, 68 First Avenue, Bush Hill Park, Enfield EN1 1BN.

Exchange & Mart. Available weekly (Thursdays) from newsagents. Includes many business opportunities, services, and goods for sale.

Daltons Weekly. Featuring property, business and investment opportunities.

Managing Your Business. Glossy magazine published by Chase Communications, 66–68 Pentonville Road, London N1 9HS. Tel: (0171) 837 9977.

Your Business: The Guide to Small Business Success. Illustrated business magazine published by Merlin Publications Ltd, Unit 14, Hove Business Centre, Fonthill Road, Hove, East Sussex BN3 6HA. Tel: (01273) 888992

INTERNET

The Complete Idiot's Guide to the Internet, Peter Kent (Prentice Hall Europe).

How to Activate Your Web Site, Bob Algie (Ziff Davis, 1998).

Internet in an Hour, Don Mayo (DDC Publishing, 1998).

How to Use the Internet, Mark E Walker (Ziff Davies, 4th edition).

Doing Business on the World Wide Web, Marni C Patterson (Ziff Davies).

Teleworking Explained, M Gray, N Hodson and G Gordon (John Wiley & Sons)

Teleworking in Brief, Mike Johnson (Butterworth/Heinemann).

Surfing Your Career, Hilary Nickell (How To Books, 2nd edition, 2001).

How to Grow Your Small Business Rapidly Online, Jim Green (How To Books).

INDEX